THE CAPTAIN'S WIFE

The Captain's Wife

Aled Eames

Adapted from Welsh by
Elinor Ellis

First published in Welsh in 1984
Adaptation in 2016

Images:
© Gwasanaeth Archifau Gwynedd
© Aled Eames Estate
© Elinor Ellis

ISBN: 978-1-84524-233-6

Cover design: Eleri Owen

Published by Gwasg Carreg Gwalch,
12 Iard yr Orsaf, Llanrwst, Wales LL26 0EH
tel: 01492 642031
email: books@carreg-gwalch.com
website: www.carreg-gwalch.com

*For my daughter, Elizabeth Helen,
and my son, Donald Richard*

Contents

Foreword to the English Adaptation

I adapted Aled Eames' book into English some years ago for the benefit of my daughter and son who are not Welsh speakers.

I must emphasise that it is not strictly a translation but an adaptation, with anecdotes of my own included in italics.

Captain Thomas Owen was a master mariner and captain of the *Cambrian Monarch* when his wife wrote the diary. Being at sea was a long and lonely experience, especially for a woman in a sailing ship; and more so if becalmed for long periods. Ellen Owen wrote the diary for her sister, Sarah. The third sister, Mary, was my paternal great grandmother. She lived in Tyddyn Mawr, Tudweiliog.

A generation later Captain Owen became a ship owner in his own right and my maternal grandfather, Captain Griffith Jones, Langdale, Pwllheli became his commodore captain. My grandmother, Ellen Jones, spent many years at sea with him. She died in 1960 aged 89, having lived with us in Liverpool for 10 years, coming after my own father died, aged 45, in 1950.

Thus, after the age of 11, I was brought up by two 'Cape Horners', both women, my mother, Moraned, having been born on the *Langdale* in 1909.

Elinor Ellis, Langdale, Bro Gwylwyr, Nefyn, Gwynedd

Preface

The reason for starting this little book was a coincidence.

Amongst a number of documents shown to me by Miss Sarah Roberts, Trelan, Pwllheli, an enthusiastic researcher into local history, was a copy she made of a diary when spending a weekend with a family member in July 1966.

At the same time a letter came to the archives from Mr Gwilym Jones, Y Felin, Tudweiliog mentioning a number of documents he had concerning his uncle.

Mr Bryn Parry, the Gwynedd archivist and I realised that the diary and the documents related to the same family, the one on the wife's side and the other on the husband's, and that the Ellen Owen who wrote the diary was the Captain's wife. We therefore went down to Tudweiliog to Y Felin to see if there was any more information to be had regarding the families of Pwllcwd, Y Felin and Minafon. We were given great co-operation, as usual, in Llŷn and Eifionydd an area that still appreciates its' maritime history.

We understood that the original diary was still in the possession of Ellen Owen's family and we are very grateful to Mrs Margery Hughes Jones for the warm welcome she gave us and to the whole family for permission to publish the diary. The diary is important because it is one of the few, indeed the only one we know of from this era, written in Welsh by a young woman who sailed the seas with her husband. We believe that through publishing it we are paying tribute to a generation of Welsh women who faced the dangers and the pleasures of sailing the world in the sailing ships on which their husbands were masters.

It is a pleasure to thank many friends who made the book possible: To Mrs Margery Hughes Jones, Nefyn; Mr Gwilym Jones, Y Felin, Tudweiliog; Mrs Llewellyn,

Graeanfryn; Morfa Nefyn, Miss Sarah Roberts,Trelan, Pwllheli and Mrs Iona Roberts, Glanrhyd, Edern. I also wish to thank for the information regarding the *Langdale* Captain John Griffith Jones, Avallon, Morfa Nefyn and Mrs Elinor Ellis, Heswall, Wirral. Mr Bryn Parry and I had a tremendous welcome in Tudweiliog school and we are very grateful to Mr Wyn Pritchard and his staff not only in allowing us to peruse the archives of the school, but also to spend a pleasant time in the school that was so close to Captain Thomas Owen's heart. It is also a pleasure to thank the staff of the registry office in Pwllheli for their time given researching the date of Thomas and Ellen Owen's marriage. My friend, Mike Stammers, curator of the Merseyside Maritime Museum and Mrs Adrian Rance, curator of Southampton Museum were kind enough to answer many questions regarding the contents of this little book. At Gwynedd Archives, Caernarfon, Miss Anne Thomas, Mr Martin Davis and Mr Robert G. Williams were a great support and Mrs Christine Williams was happy to decipher my untidy writing, type and retype with exceptional patience, and I am really grateful to them. My old friend, Mr T. M. Basset was very kind looking at the script and he searched many documents, but, of course, I am the only one responsible for any mistakes. I am well used by now to tending my thanks to Mr Bryn Parry for his untiring support regarding many maritime books, and his contribution to this little book was enormous, visiting the area, discussing and comparing and sharing with me the ambience and experiences of Thomas and Ellen Owen's life.

Indeed, his name should go down as co-author. I hope he has enjoyed Thomas and Ellen Owen's company as much as I have. He knows how much I owe him over many years.

Aled Eames, Moelfre, Anglesey

Chapter 1

Roots

On a cold, foggy morning in January, with the strong, west wind pounding the surf onto the rocks of Porth Ysgaden, it was easy for Bryn Parry and myself to imagine the feelings of Ellen and Thomas Owen when they returned home from their travels more than 100 years ago. Their remains now lie in the churchyard of St Cwyfan in Tudweiliog under a tall, brown, marble tombstone, all prearranged by Thomas before he died. Captain Thomas Owen was a methodical man.

On a stormy morning earlier this year it was a clear, but imagined picture that was in my mind. It was of a strong,

Captain Thomas Owen when captain of the British India, *1874-1880*

muscular boy running barefooted in and out of the waves on the beach at Porth Ysgaden about 1855. Maybe it was a stormy morning like ours or maybe it was still with the sea mist swallowing the boy up. Maybe on a quiet, moonlit night the picture is deceptively clear, as more than 100 years have passed since then. It is very likely that Thomas and his compatriots who went to sea from Nefyn, Edern, Porthdinllaen and Tudweiliog played on the schooners which brought coal to these beaches, and were thus well used to managing boats from early childhood. It is unlikely that

Ellen, although she was the same age as Thomas, would have been at Porth Ysgaden as often, as she was the daughter of Pwllcwd, Llaniestyn, on the eastern side of the Cefnamwlch estate. She and her sisters might come to Porth Ysgaden on an occasional sunny day or to see the results of a great storm like the one that sank the *Royal Charter* in October 1859. This is when the schooner *Weaver* was wrecked at Tudweiliog together with the Spanish ship *Vella* and 9 schooners were lost with all hands at Porth Colman.[1] All the local children would head for the beach at times like this and it might have been then that Thomas first set eyes on the young woman who was to sail the world with him on the ship *Cambrian Monarch* starting in 1881/2. All the story can do at the moment is to trace their roots.

Sarah Williams, Tyddyn Sander, the sister for whom Ellen Owen wrote her diary. Sarah died in 1906

In the Llaniestyn parish records the christening of the children of Richard and Elinor Williams, Pyllacydach farm is recorded. Catherine, June 11th 1837; Margery, November 8th 1838; Sarah, September 22nd 1840; Mary, November 7th 1842. There is no sign of Ellen's name. In the Tudweiliog register we have records of other children born to Richard and Elinor Williams but their home is now called Pwllcwd. Jane, 1st October 1848; Anne, 13th February 1853; Morris, 28th October 1855. On the other side of the coin we have the register of deaths; so many died in childhood: 7th December 1849 Jane Williams, Pwllcwd, aged 2; 6th May 1856, Margery Williams, Pwllancydach, aged 17; 23rd September 1856, Anne Williams, Pwllau Cydach, aged 3; 5th October 1857, Jane Williams, Pwllau Cydach, aged 7; 12th October. 1857, Morris Williams, Pwllau Cydach aged 2; 14th November 1857 Catherine Williams, Pwllcwd aged 20: and then as was the world for women at that time the mother followed her children to the grave, aged 67 on March 4th 1880. By this time the family had moved to Tyddyn Sander, a much smaller place, as Richard was suffering from rheumatism and was being looked after by his unmarried daughter, Sarah, and the servant, David Jones, aged 15 from Benllech.[2]

What, therefore, of Ellen, who was so diligent in writing her diary on board the *Cambrian Monarch* for her sisters, Sarah, at home in Tyddyn Sander caring for their father, and Mary, married and living in Tyddyn Mawr. *(We used to go to Tyddyn Mawr for tea and, as was the fashion then, it was an enormous afternoon tea consisting of bread and butter with jam, never sandwiches; pancakes that were the size of a side plate with butter and jam, about 6 each; custard tart, which was never a favourite with me, sandwich cake, fruit cake; maybe bara brith, maybe scones. This was in the 1940/50s. I loved those teas; and there was always lots of family round a big mahogany table in the dining room. A table like ours in Heswall. We all ate lots! It was Uncle Robert and Aunty Lisa who were there then but I called them 'Ewyrth Robert a Modryb Lisa.')*

Ellen was born in Pwllcyd in 1845/6. Her father was described in the 1851 census as being a farmer employing 7 labourers, and Pyllarcydarch as a farm of 260 acres. Those members of the family at home on the night of the census were Ellin (i.e. Elinor) the mother and Richard's wife, aged 38 and daughters, Catherine, 13; Margery, 12; Sarah 10; Ellen, 5; Jane 6 months. There were also 2 maids, Mary Thomas aged 29 born in Llanbedrog, and Elizabeth Jones,

The Pwllcwd family: Richard and Ellen Williams and their daughters
Sarah (on the left), Mary (in the centre) and Ellen, the writer of the diary

aged 19, from Llaniestyn, together with 5 unmarried farm labourers; Thomas Jones, 21, Tudweiliog; Elias Jones, 19, Bryncroes; Hugh Jones, 16, Ceidio; John Jones, 15, Llaniestyn; David Williams, 14, Edern.

Ten years later Richard Williams was still farming at Pwllcwd, but only he and his wife plus 2 daughters were at home on the night of the census. As mentioned previously many of the children had died and Ellen was not at home. Sarah, aged 20 and Mary, aged 18, were included in the census. There was one visitor and 5 different labourers, 2 described as cowmen, plus one maid. What about Ellen? She had probably already moved to Pwllheli to private school to avoid the sickness which had taken her only brother and her sisters.

We have very little knowledge about Ellen in these early years and there is no certainty about the school in Pwllheli, but in the 1840s and 50s Pwllheli was an important centre, not only for agriculture but also for ship building. More than 50 wooden ships were built there between 1845 and 1870. Amongst them were many that became famous in the maritime history of Gwynedd; e.g. the full rigged ships *Ancient Briton* and the *William Carey*; the brig *John Arthur Pritchard* and the schooner *Twelve Apostles*, which made a name for herself in the Porthmadog slate trade.[3] This suggests that Ellen, as a schoolgirl in Pwllheli, had the opportunity to become as familiar with the world of shipping as with that of farming. As we think of her background as the daughter of a large farm and her experiences on the *Cambrian Monarch* and later in Minafon, crocheting, sewing and knitting to a very high standard, one can surmise that it was to one of the schools for young ladies from families of means that Ellen went, such as mentioned in 'Gentlewoman'.[4]

A great deal of this is surmise, but the 1871 census shows that by now only Sarah and Ellen are at home in Pwllcwd, and that Mary has married William Williams, Tyddyn Mawr.

When I started writing this book I had no idea when Ellen was married, but the staff of the Pwllheli registry office solved the problem for me. I can therefore imagine the fuss going on in Pwllcwd in the spring of 1876. Thomas Owen had passed captain, and had completed his first voyage as master to South America on the large ship *British India*. The wedding is noted in the *Baner ac Amserau Cymru*. On June 15th 1876, at Salem chapel, Pwllheli, by the Reverend R. Thomas, Tudweiliog, Captain Thomas Owen, the *British India* and Miss Ellen Williams, Pwllcwd.[5] That is all we know. Captain Owen sailed on the *British India* as captain until 1880, but we do not know whether Ellen went with him during those years. We do know that in 1881, according to the census again, she and her husband were at his family home, Y Felin, Tudweiliog. They were about to leave on a voyage aboard the *Cambrian Monarch*. It is now time to turn our attention to the family of Captain Thomas Owen.

Not far from the main road between Nefyn and Aberdaron, on the sea side of Tudweiliog stands the mill, home to Owen Owen, the miller and his wife, Ann. In 1851 Owen Owen was 34 years old, born in the parish of Penllech, farmed 13 acres, employed 2 labourers, and had a wife 2 years older than himself. They had 4 children; Owen, aged 10; Thomas, aged 4; Ann, aged 2; and 2 month old baby, Richard.

Thomas Owen's application for his mate's ticket is in the National Maritime Museum at Greenwich. It is in his own handwriting and confirms his age, gives his address as Tudweiliog Mill and his date of birth as 25th November 1847. There is no information as to Thomas's early years, but one can assume that he spent his time helping around the mill, frequenting Tudweiliog school and running with the village boys past the mill, through the fields and farms, Tŷ Hir and Porthysgaden, to the beaches of Towyn, Porth Ysgaden, Porth Gwylan and Porth Ychen or walking over the rocks of Penrhyn Melyn and watching the ships unloading coal at Porth Colmon. His father is seen to be quite affluent but it is the eldest son, Owen, who trains as a miller, and therefore it is not surprising that it was Thomas, along with other younger sons of Llŷn farmers, who would exchange the hard life of the land for the hard life of the sea. The Gwynedd archives show that Thomas took his first ship, as did hundreds of Llŷn boys, typically for this period in Gwynedd maritime history, on the quay at Caernarfon on June 6th 1863, aged 13.

The captain of the *Antelope*[6] was Owen Roberts, aged 43, from Nefyn, a man about the same age as Thomas's father. They may, indeed, have been neighbours as well as contemporaries. Mariners often put Nefyn for the locality in which they were born or even Caernarfon or Anglesey. Owen Roberts was the managing owner of the *Antelope*, an 83 ton schooner built in Nefyn in 1828 and many of the Nefyn inhabitants held shares in her in the 1860s. The mate was Robert Owens, aged 35, from Nefyn; the experienced mariner was Ellis Lewis, aged 23, from Pwllheli; the 2 ordinary seamen, Owen Jones, 21, from Conway; Robert Williams, aged 17, from Morfa. Then comes the entry 'Thomas Owen, 16, Penllech, first entry, cook'. I wonder whether Thomas had shown something of the adventurous spirit that was indicative of the years ahead, and added 3 years to his age in order to become a sailor on the *Antelope*. It was quite likely that he was a big, strong lad and no-one worried about his age. The *Antelope* sailed on the same day Thomas Owen joined her, and he would be familiarising himself with the rigging and the galley as the walls of Caernarfon Castle disappeared in the distance, and the maritime career of the miller's son began.

Naturally the *Antelope* carried slates, and on May 17th, eleven days after crossing the Caernarfon bar, she unloaded these in London.

Within a week they had acquired another cargo which, although there were no documents, could possibly have been cement, a common enough cargo to carry from London northwards, and they sailed for Liverpool on June 25th, arriving on July 18th. Thomas went home for a spell and then, on September 28th he boarded another slate ship in the Menai Straits, this time as an able seaman on the *Lady Louisa Pennant*, one of the Port Penrhyn schooners, built in Bangor by John Parry.[7] By this time she belonged to the Ellis family, the descendants of another well known Bangor builder, Edward Ellis, and close friend of Captain Thomas Williams of Liverpool, the founder of the company that

Thomas Owen was to serve in for many years to come. After a voyage of a few months, finishing on 5th March 1864 Thomas Owen left the *Lady Louisa Pennant* and on March 17th joined one of the Menai Straits slate ships, the schooner *Collina*.[8] John Owen of Nefyn was the operating owner and Robert Owen his son, aged 32, the master. She had arrived in Port Penrhyn from Garston at the end of February and the crew paid off. The new crew consisted of Robert Jones, the mate, from Nefyn, Thomas Owen, A.B. and Richard Hughes, ordinary seaman and cook from Beaumaris. They sailed for Shoreham on the 18th March, arriving at the end of the month, and sailing from there to Runcorn at the beginning of April and back to the Straits on May 11th where Thomas Owen left her to join the *Profit and Loss*, a well known schooner built in Nefyn and registered in London.[9] Thomas Owen spent 20 months on this ship. (On St. David's Day a Welsh lady living near the Thames puts daffodils on the grave of a young sailor from Nefyn. He died on the *Profit and Loss* and was buried near where the schooner unloaded her slates.)

By 1866 Thomas Owen was ready to move to the larger Liverpool sailing ships in order to gain experience of square riggers, and also to get his mate and master's certificates. He sat his mate's certificate in December 1869,[10] the 'only mate' certificate, which was useful in the coastal trade, but he needed more experience. He therefore sailed as second mate on the *Lady Belleau*, a wooden barque built in Quebec and owned by a Nefyn man. He gained his first mate's certificate in July 1871 and his master's certificate for square riggers in February 1873. The master of the barque *Alcoats* wrote a letter of congratulation to him in April of that year regarding his efforts as senior officer on that ship over the previous 15 months. During that time 'he conducted himself with sobriety and was a first class seaman, at all times energetic, steady, sober and honest'.[11] The reason he left this ship was to work on his master's certificate.

Although he had now passed captain, Thomas Owen had to wait patiently for his first command and he looked for a position as first officer. This is when he met Captain Thomas Williams. By 1873 this master mariner, born in Llandwrog[12] twenty years before Thomas Owen, was one of the owners of one of the most profitable sailing ship companies in Liverpool, and managed a fleet of ships which had previously belonged to the Black Ball line, appointing some of Liverpool's best captains as their masters, nearly all of whom were Welsh speaking Welshmen from Gwynedd.

The *British India* was a wooden, full rigged ship, 190ft. long, 38.3ft. beam and 23.9ft. deep, built by Goss of New Brunswick in 1862 and bought by Thomas Williams company from her first owners in 1873. She cost £12,000. Due to the American civil war the British markets enlarged[13] and there was a demand for ships in the seventies.

By this time the company were running 8 large wooden ships, several of which were ex Black Ball line ships. These had been bought from James Baines & Co., and there was no problem in finding backers in the Welsh Calvanistic Methodist community for that venture. The same occurred with the 2 later ships, the *British India*, and the *Eastern Light* all known to be good, sound ships.

They were all insured with the marine insurance companies of Nefyn and Pwllheli. In February 1873 Captain Thomas Williams became chairman of the various companies following his partner William Roberts the previous president, who died in 1872. The importance of the part played by the well to do Welsh in Liverpool and London in supporting the insurance companies of Nefyn and Pwllheli is a story in itself.[14]

When Thomas Owen was promoted to first mate on the

British India on his first voyage for Thomas Williams' company, he had obtained a position with a firm that was very highly thought of in North Wales and Liverpool. Amongst the investors in this company there were not only the captains described, such as Captain Richard Richards[15] of Barmouth, but also well to do merchants and capitalists from the Welsh speaking community. In this environment Thomas Owen's maritime, social and religious background was a tremendous advantage. The impression one gets from looking at the article and the crew agreement lists was that captains, managers and even ordinary seamen stayed with this company longer than with other Welsh companies. There is room to suppose that Captain Thomas Williams and his maritime managers were like his brother-in-law, Captain William Griffith of Port Dinorwig, in that they looked after their men very well. Thomas Owen, therefore, looked forward to showing Captain Thomas Williams what calibre of mate he had appointed to the *British India*.

Thomas Owen joined the *British India* in Liverpool in April 1873[16] a few weeks after she became available to the Welsh company, and we can imagine him walking the decks checking the rigging and all the gear, making sure it was absolutely right before his first voyage for his new owners. The master was Captain Evan Roberts, most likely from the same background as Thomas Owen. The *British India* sailed from Liverpool about two months after Thomas Owen had passed his full rigged ships' master's certificate, and he clearly made a good impression on Captain Roberts on the way out and on the return voyage. They reached Le Havre from Bombay on September 9th 1874 and on 21st October Captain Roberts wrote a letter to his superiors recommending Thomas Owen: 'This is to certify that Thomas Owen served on the above named ship under my command from 12th April 1873 to the above date. I have

Captain Thomas Owen, ship's captain and later shipowner of Minafon, Tudweiliog

always found him to be a careful, industrious and sober officer and have recommended him as master of the *British India*, or anyone who requires his services.'[17]

Captain Thomas Williams took note of this favourable reference from Captain Evan Roberts and as a result Captain Thomas Owen sailed as master of the *British India* from 1874 to 1880. As luck would have it the death of Captain William Roberts in 1872 and of Captain Owen Williams in 1874 created a gap in the company hierarchy that was an advantage to Captain Thomas Owen in the eighties. Captain Owen Williams was younger than his brother, Captain Thomas Williams, and had passed his master's certificate at the age of 21.[18] He was married to the daughter of Reverend Hugh Hughes, Beaumaris, and died in the Indian ocean on board the *William Leavitt*, the ship of which he was master. He planned to come home after this voyage in order to look after the family business so that his older brother could spend some time in his second home, Parciau, Cricieth. Things did not turn out like that and his body was brought home to be buried in Anglesey soil in Beaumaris. He was well known for the financial support he elicited from all over the world for the building of an English Presbyterian church in Beaumaris, which was the project of his older brother Thomas and his wife Jane. In 1880 this captain also died, leaving even greater gaps in the company hierarchy, thus favouring the promotion of Captain Thomas Owen at the age of 33. Indeed, Captain Owen might well have been imagining the possibility of becoming a partner in the company before long and thence a shipowner in his own right. It was another 10 years before he realised his ambition.

I only have anecdotal information about Thomas Owen as master of the *British India*. In August 1875 Captain Robert Thomas, Llandwrog wrote interestingly from Pabellon de Pica[19] on the south east coast of South America describing a meeting on the *Malabar* which belonged to the William Thomas line of Liverpool. Captain Davies Evans, Nefyn, master of the *Malabar* was highly thought of amongst the Welsh seafaring community and many influential people met each other on his ship. There was much call for guano in the seventies for fertilising Europe's fields and hundreds of large sailing ships waited at anchor, sometimes for months on unhospitable shores, to load this stinking cargo. Robert Thomas wrote to his fiancée that there were more than a hundred empty ships like his, the *Glentilt*, waiting at Port Lobos in August 1875. This is part of his letter, written in full in the book *Shipmaster*, the story of Robert Thomas:

'... This place is a new deposit and therefore they are very backward with the works. There are more than 100 vessels here now, most of them empty like the *Glentilt*.

You will be surprised to hear that I am now a great teetotler. Some Americans started a meeting, signing not to drink any spirits nor any intoxicating drink whilst on this coast. So the Welsh started another and so now every Welsh captain and most of the officers and many of their men signed this pledge and we hold a meeting every week. There are 15 Welsh ships here. Your humble servant is one of the conductors, but I would sign for only 6 months for you are aware that I have always been very steady and it is to benefit others that I have joined at all. Great good it may do them I say...'

One of the Welsh ships was the *British India* with Thomas Owen on his first voyage as master, and he was one of the Welsh masters who listened to and shared the evenings on the *British India* described in Robert Thomas' book, and who was at the meeting on the *Malabar* held on that still evening in August 1875. David Evans and Robert Thomas conducted the meeting, as was shown in the programme that the latter sent home,[20] with several Captains taking part, including Thomas Owen.

PROGRAMME
Temperance meeting on board ship *Malabar* Wed. evening at 7p.m.

Conductors.   Captn. Evans & Captn. Thomas
                Captn. Davies *Teresa* Chairman
1. Hymn & prayer by O. Roberts, *Glentilt*
2. Speech by Captn. Owen, *B. India*
3. Song ('Come to the Mountains') *Teresa* choir
4. Speech by E. Evans, *Glentilt*
5. ('Ash Grove') *Malabar* choir
6. Speech by Mr Edwards, *Dusty Miller*
7. Anthem ('Glory to God in the highest') *Teresa* choir
8. Song ('Gwendolen Pugh'), Captain Thomas, *Glentilt*
9. Speech by Captn. Roberts, *Duke of Rothsey*
10. Song ('Annie Lizie') Miss Williams, *Eastern Light*
11. Address Captain Evans, *Malabar*
12. Hymn & prayer H. Williams, *Leonore*
                God Save the Queen

Notice also that two of the ships mentioned, the *British India* and the *Eastern Light*, belonged to Thomas Williams and Co. and that Captain Williams' daughter was on board the *Eastern Light*.

There was another little anecdote regarding Captain Thomas Owen on the south west coast, as the south east coast of America was known in the Welsh maritime towns and villages. A large number of sailing ships were caught in the war between Chile and Peru 1879–1884. The bone of contention was the wealth that emanated from the nitrate and guano trade, and the refusal of Chile to allow Peru to control it. In April 1879 Chile started a blockade of the Peruvian ports and Captain Robert Thomas in the *British Princess*, for example, remained in Callao bay from April 17th to October 22nd 1879 before sailing for Lobos d'Afuera, six hundred miles north. His diary reports:

'... I stayed in Cardiff for about two weeks this time and then sailed for Callao with a cargo of coals and made good passage out. But when I got out I found that the Peruvians were at war with Chile, and on account of this I layed in Callao bay for about 6 months, and then went down to Lobos d'Afuera, about 600 miles north of Callao, to load guano. But when we had about 600 tons on board, the Chilean authorities came and put a stop to it all by setting fire to the shoots and taking all the launches away and setting fire to them.

We all (Shipmasters) went on board the Admiral's ship and begged hard to finish our loading, but he said his orders were to destroy the loading facilities, which he did. They afterwards sailed away and providentially the next morning almost all the launches were recovered, for although holes had been made in them and some of them fired by means of paraffin oil still they did not sink,

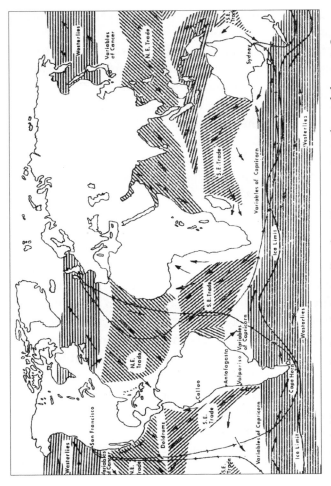

Probable routes of sailing ships travelling from Europe to Australia and thence to San Francisco and back to Europe.

Ellen Owen's voyage on the Cambrian Monarch, 1881/1882

and everybody put out their boats to save the launches and which was accomplished.

The fire about the shoots was also put out and in a week's time everything was again ready for loading. But the Governer of the island would not allow us to load till he had communicated with the Government. So the answer in time came not to go on loading till further notice. This was a great blow to us, but could not be helped, and I, in company with 2 other shipmasters went over to Etten, a little town on the mainland, and from which we could wire to Callao for instructions, and in the meantime all the ships sent their crews on shore to collect stone ballast and carry some on board in case we had to go to another place. This was hard and tedious work for they had to roll the stones down from the top of the hills and break them etc...'

Thus Captain Thomas and two other masters had to go ashore to Etten, on the mainland, in order to get permission through Callao; their crews in the meantime lugging rocks from the shore as ballast for the ships in case they had to leave the area in a hurry, being unable to load their ships with the guano cargo. The *British Princess* and the *True Briton* (Captain Edwards, Caernarfon), both ships belonging to Davies of Borth, were there until March 1880 before loading a cargo. Captain Thomas' ship reached Falmouth six days before the *True Briton*.

Captain Thomas Owen was also in this area at the time of the Peruvian/Chilean war. He managed to load a cargo of nitrates and leave in time to arrive in Dunkirk by December 13th 1879; some months before the majority of masters.[21] The biographer reported the following:

'... At the time of the Peruvian and Chilean war, he

succeeded in entering the port of Mexilliones, Peru, while blockaded by the Chilean navy, and loaded a cargo of nitrates, a daring achievement which was highly commented on at the time by the British and continental press.'

At that time there were so few cargoes coming to Europe from South America that Thomas Owen would have obtained an excellent price for the nitrates, and it was after this that he was made master of the *Cambrian Monarch*. Captain David Hughes (ex Black Ball line) had been her captain since she was launched in 1876, the first of the Cambrian line. It is now time for us to look more closely at the ship on which Ellen sailed and which provides the background to her diary.

Chapter 2

The Cambrian Monarch

The engineering shop at the T. R. Oswald shipyard on the river Itchen close to the ferry in Woolston, Southampton, was known as 'the slaughter house'. It was not, therefore, surprising that Jimmy Angel's mother was worried about him as he started his apprenticeship there in 1883. Jimmy Angel remembers well the excessive activity of the yard in the eighties with the tremendous demand for sailing ships and steamers, and the engineers with nothing to hand for any negligent individual who lost an arm or leg. Sometimes chunks of iron or parts of blocks fell from the tops of the spars killing one of the workers. They worked from six in the morning until five at night with half an hour at midday to have a bite to eat. No-one was allowed to have anything to drink whether tea, coffee or beer or to smoke on the yard. They were a tough crowd, mostly from the north-east, the Tyne, or from Scotland, from the Clyde yards. They enjoyed playing football in their spare time or greyhound racing on Peartree green. These are the people who started the Labour movement and the co-operatives in South Wales and who were the star turns in the silver bands.[1]

Seven years before Jimmy Angel started work in the Oswald shipyard, the first and smallest of the fleet belonging to the Captain Thomas Williams company of Liverpool was built; the *Cambrian Monarch*. The middle seventies were important times of change in the history of shipbuilding in Britain, when there were technological advances resulting in large iron ships being built to satisfy the needs of the business community, who were now involved in the European wars and the American civil war. The trend in the eighties then was for building small wooden ships in the local yards such as in Porthmadog and Amlwch but also seeking to buy large, second hand, wooden ships from America, and new, large iron ships off the stocks from Liverpool, Glasgow and north-east England. The Davies company at Borth bought from Roydens in Liverpool; William Thomas, Liverpool, bought from Doxfords in Sunderland and at R. and J. Evans, Liverpool; The Gwynedd Company and the Eryri Company bought from Doxfords. Captain Thomas Williams, however, went to one of the best builders in Britain, T. R. Oswald of Southampton.

One of the most well-known, forward looking and adventurous men of the Victorian age was Thomas Ridley Oswald, builder of hundreds of iron ships. Having started in Sunderland in the sixties and seventies, and from 1876 to 1888 in Southampton, he ended up in Wales, in Aberdaugleddau (Milford Haven), where large ships such as the *Speke* and the *Ditton* were built. It is said that Oswald was very successful in Sunderland where he built 149 ships, but he moved in 1876 to Woolston's yard in Southampton taking a large number of his workforce with him. They left the Castletown housing estate which had been built by Oswald to house them. In the first year there Oswald had his first commission for an iron ship from Captain Thomas Williams, the precursor of many for that company, each one of which carried the name Cambrian. It is not certain to this day who designed the Cambrian ships but it could well have been Hercules Linton, who designed the *Cutty Sark*. Certainly the *Cambrian Monarch* was a beautiful ship with good lines, elegant form, and well balanced masts. She was certainly a fine sailer as described by Ellen Owen in her diary some years after she was launched.

Monday. March 20th 1882[2]
We have had a strong breeze since the tow, but not too
strong. It is a fair wind. There is another ship in sight
today. I have written every day since we sailed, although
the ship rolls and pitches sometimes, she rides the sea
well, being quite narrow. It was snowing yesterday and
there were heavy squalls, and the same today. It is quite
cold. We should have rounded the Horn by this time
next week. This is what we have achieved since tow. 216.
(i.e. days out)

The *Cambrian Monarch* was slightly smaller in length,
breadth, and depth of hold space than the majority of iron
ships commissioned by the shipowners of Liverpool and
North Wales in the seventies, and much smaller than those
of the eighties and nineties. To give today's reader some
comparison here is a list of Cambrian ships (see pages 42 to
45) and some other well-known ships belonging to North
Walian shipowners. As an extra measure I include the *Cutty
Sark* which can be seen at Greenwich and the *Wavertree*
built by Oswald of Woolston, Southampton, which can be
seen in New York.

The photograph of the *Cambrian Monarch* shows a
typical sailing ship of the seventies, carrying square sails on
three masts, and therefore known as a full rigged ship. As
time went on there was call for larger ships to carry larger
cargoes. Thus in the eighties we saw the four masted
barques like the *Principality* and the *Metropolis* (*and Taid's*
Grenada), and full rigged ships like the *Cambrian Princess*. In
the nineties the steel ships were larger still. In his book *The
Last of the Windjammers* Basil Lubbock compares the sail
measurement of six ships belonging to Welsh shipowners in
Liverpool. In the picture we can see that the *Cambrian
Monarch* is at anchor, having unloaded her cargo, and that

she is very high in the water. Looking at the stern of the ship you see the poop which is where the Captain's wife made her home during voyages. Think then of Ellen Owen (*and Nain Langdale*) making a voyage almost confined to this part of the ship; but remember, too, that it was very much more comfortable than many a home on land.

As so many ships were built in the seventies and eighties we have a good idea of their furnishings from the builders inventories, and if you go on board the *Cutty Sark* at Greenwich, you will see the Captain's quarters.

It is probable that the *Cambrian Monarch* was easier to manage at sea than some of the larger ships that came after her. It is said that she was less likely to be affected by a following sea, but that would actually depend on the nature of her cargo, the way it was stowed and the state of the sea and the weather. Photographs show that the *Cambrian Monarch* was similar to her sister ships and Thomas Williams would have been well pleased with his new ship. Exactly as the master craftsmen of the wooden ships of Porthmadog, Porthdinllaen, Nefyn and Newquay created ships' mascots on the bow of their ships, so did the English shipbuilders take pride in their craft. It is more than likely that the figurehead of the *Cambrian Monarch* was carved in wood by Dick Cowell. The photograph of the figurehead that he carved for the *Cambrian Chieftain* is seen in many shipping books. It is, however, unlikely that a religious meeting would have been held at the launching of the *Monarch*, as would have happened in Caernarfon or Porthdinllaen, but Captain Thomas Williams and his co-investors would have been present, watching her ride at anchor on the river Itchen and listening to the music of the shipyard's silver band.

Who, then, were these investors? Although the company statutes of 1862 and 1867 encouraged many

North Wales ship owners to form limited companies where you could buy shares for £10 or £50, Thomas Williams' company belonged to the old school, and so it was until the 1890s, and twenty years after his death. It was the tradition, indeed the law before limited companies came into existence, for the financing of a ship to be divided into 64 shares. It was deemed that 4 sixty-fourths signified ownership. In the early days the captain and the builder would be the main 'owners', with many a ship belonging to the captain and, for example, his father or his sister, and his father might have been a farmer. Later, the local shopkeepers and the publican or the minister would be included in the venture. As the ships became larger still they were more expensive, and it was necessary to move away from a locality to seek shareholders, but there was never any shortage of would-be owners in North Wales. The expansion of shipping and the introduction of the railways saw a period of prosperity coming to North Wales as the quarrymen invested in the ships in the hope of making their fortune ("My ship's come in"). Although the smaller coastal ships had shareholders from the quarries, larger ships as owned by William Roberts and Thomas Williams needed wealthy shareholders with plenty of backing. Obviously Liverpool was a great source of finance as half of that city was built by Welshmen from Arfon and Anglesey. *(See book entitled 'The Welsh builders of Liverpool' by J. W. Jones, Cintra, who went to Heathfield Road chapel with us.)* Most of these builders had learnt their craft as ships' carpenters and their background was similar to those also giving financial backing, the Welsh speaking Welsh families of North Wales. Looking at the register of shareholders it is possible to see patterns of names as each shipowner had his personal backers.

When the *Cambrian Monarch* was registered in Liverpool on the 26th September 1876, Thomas Williams owned 64 shares. The next day he sold 4 sixty-fourths to 'Thomas Davies, Ysputty' co. Denbighshire, shipowner; 4 sixty-fourths to 'Thomas Gee, Denbigh', publisher; 4 sixty-fourths to 'Laura Williams, widow, Cricieth', and 4 sixty-fourths to 'Thomas Williams, shipowner, Denbigh'. On the 28th September he sold 4 sixty-fourths to 'Edward Ellis, Bangor, Master mariner', 4 sixty-fourths to 'D. Hughes, Caernarfon, Master mariner' (the first captain of the *Cambrian Monarch*), and on the 29th September 4 sixty-fourths to 'William Thomas Parker, Welshpool, esq'. At the beginning of October 4 sixty-fourths went each to Robert Biddy Jones, a Liverpool merchant, to Joseph Green Bayley, shipowner of Lancaster, and Humphreys Lewis, merchant, Llanrwst. On October 8th 8 sixty-fourths went to one of Thomas William's first backers, Lewis Lewis, a Caernarfon merchant. On looking at the ownership list of the other ships i.e. the *Cambrian Prince* and the *Cambrian Princess*, plus the *Cambrian Queen* and the *Cambrian Duchess* (the latter being bought from the Arvon shipping company when she was called the *Arvonia*) and also those purchased from William Roberts and Thomas Williams at the time of the collapse of the James Baines, it seems that the company relied on people who had been, and people who still were master mariners, as backers, including their own masters; and also on Welsh shareholders like Thomas Gee, Denbigh, Elis Roberts, solicitor, Llanllyfni, and Lewis Lewis of Caernarfon. Lewis was an important Caernarfon businessman, owner of the shop 'Nelson' and a good friend of Captain Thomas Williams' family for many years. When the latter died in 1880 the *Caernarvon and Denbigh Herald* recorded that one of the chief mourners at the funeral in Liverpool was Alderman Lewis Lewis, Mayor of Caernarfon.[3] A few years after this the Mercantile Navy List recorded the managing owner of many of the Cambrian

Ship, 'CAMBRIAN MONARCH,'

THOMAS WILLIAMS, COMMANDER.

Cambrian Monarch, *the full rigged ship that was home to Ellen Owen on her voyage from San Francisco to Limerick in 1882*

Fully rigged 3-masted sailing ship, Langdale. Painted by Henry Mohrmann in Antwerp. Note the captain and his wife on the poop.

Captain Thomas Owen, Captain of the Cambrian Monarch *and the* Cambrian Princess *in San Francisco*

Captain and Mrs Thomas Owen in Hamburg

On board Langdale *in Australia. Captain and Mrs Griffith Jones with John and Moraned*

Captain and Mrs Thomas Owen and the crew of the Cambrian Monarch
in San Francisco in 1882
(see reference p. 150; The Diary: Page 67 [6])

Langdale *in distress. Damage to masts and spars*

Captain Griffiths Jones as an able seaman
(2nd left, next to back row)

Captain Griffith Jones (seated) with his first mate, Captain Kingham on
board Langdale

Captain and Mrs Griffith Jones with their son, John,
taken in San Francisco

Captain Griffith Jones with his
daughter, Moraned, in Rio

Mrs Ellen Jones with her two
children, John and Moraned

The grave of Captain Thomas Owen FRGS at St Cwyfan's churchyard, Tudweiliog

ships as Mrs Jane Lewis, the widow of Captain Thomas Williams, who had now married Lewis Lewis, the shop owner.

Thomas Gee also kept in contact with the Cambrian ships. He took 4 sixty-fourth shares in the *Cambrian Prince* when she was registered in 1877, and by the nineties when she was re-registered as a single ship company, he was one of a group who took shares in the *Cambrian Monarch* and the *Cambrian Prince*. The solicitor who represented the company, and other Cambrian ships, was the Thomas Gee company of Liverpool,4 one of the family of printers and publishers aforementioned. Captain Thomas Williams probably met Thomas Gee when the former was a master with the Davies of Borth company in the fifties and according to the literature he read a great deal of Welsh and was very keen to be part of the migration of which Thomas Gee was at the forefront. Thomas Williams wrote an article for *Y Traethodydd* (Travels) in 1859 on his voyage to Australia in one of the Davies ships and mentions the new venture of the 'Gwyddoniadur' (Encyclopaedia). With so much interest in the Liverpool Welsh community and his involvement with the Calvinistic Methodists and the Liberals and also with the North and South Wales bank, it is not surprising that Captain Williams and Thomas Gee were also partners in merchant shipping. Amongst the names of contributors to the building of Princes Road Welsh Calvinistic Methodist chapel, in both 1865 and 1870, was that of Captain Thomas Williams, Berkley Street.

Eleazer Roberts was another shareholder in the Cambrian ships, first assistant to the Liverpool town clerk and a well known Welsh singer. He wrote many an article for *Y Traethodydd*, *Y Drysorfa* and *Y Geninen* and laterly, under the pseudonym 'Meddyliwr' for the *Faner*. Maybe this interest in astronomy is what brought him to the notice of

Details of wellknown ships

Name	Rig	Reg.Ton.	Lgth.	Brdth.	Dpth.
Cambrian Monarch	F.R.S. Iron	1306	216.5	37	23
Cambrian Prince	F.R.S. Iron	1349	224.7	37.1	22.6
Cambrian Princess (I)	F.R.S. Iron	1350	224.7	37.1	22.6
Cambrian Queen (ex Hoogly)	Barque Iron	1300	221.7	36.8	22.8
Cambrian Chieftain	Barque Iron	1492	230	37.5	22.5
Cambrian King	F.R.S. Steel	1718	260.4	38.2	23.1
Cambrian Hills	F.R.S. Steel	1760	260.7	38.1	23.1
Cambrian Warrior (ex Miltiades)	Barque Steel	1432	230.6	37.0	21.8
Cambrian Princess (II)	F.R.S. Iron	2437	305	41.3	25
Anglesey	F.R.S. Iron	1297	219	38.3	23
Merioneth	F.R.S. Iron	1408	231.4	38.9	23.6
Ogwen	F.R.S. Iron	1381	231.0	36.1	22.0
Menai	F.R.S. Iron	1434	231.1	36.2	22
Principality	Barque Iron 4m	1758	258.5	39.6	23.1
Kate Thomas	F.R.S. Iron	1748	258.0	39.5	23.1
Dominion	Barque Steel 4m	2539	294.0	43.0	24.0
Gwynedd	Barque Iron	1053	204.6	34.6	21.2

Built	*By*	*Owner*
Southampton 1876	T. R. Oswald	T. Williams & Co.
Southampton 1876	T. R. Oswald	T. Williams & Co.
Southampton 1877	T. R. Oswald	T. Williams & Co.
Sunderland 1868	Oswald & Co.	T. Williams & Co.
Sunderland 1885	Osbourne Graham & Co.	T. Williams & Co.
Glasgow Port 1890	Russell & Co.	T. Williams & Co.
Glasgow Port 1892	A. Rodger & Co.	T. Williams & Co.
Sunderland 1885	J. Laing	T. Williams & Co.
Southampton 1884	Oswald, Mordaunt & Co.	T. Williams & Co.
Liverpool 1875	T. B. Royden	Hughes (i.e. Davies, Menai Bridge)
Liverpool 1875	T. B. Royden	Hughes (i.e. Davies, Menai Bridge)
Sunderland 1880	R. Foster	Arfon Shipping Co.
Co.Sunderland 1880	R. Foster	Arfon Shipping Co. (then W. Thomas, Liverpool)
Sunderland 1885	Doxford	W. Thomas, Liverpool
Sunderland 1885	Doxford	W. Thomas, Liverpool
Sunderland 1891	Doxford	W. Thomas, Liverpool
Sunderland 1877	Osbourne Graham	N. Wales Shipping Co.

Name	Rig	Reg.Ton.	Lgth.	Brdth.	Dpth.
Eivion	Barque Iron	1153	211.1	35.0	21.8
Moel Eilian	Barque Iron	1081	221.5	35.0	21.2
Moel y Don	Barque Iron	1080	222.0	35.0	21.2
Moel Tryvan	Barque Iron	1691	258.0	38.0	23.1
County of Anglesea	Barque Iron	1103	214.4	35.2	21.2
Criccieth Castle	F.R.S. Iron	1920	263.9	39.0	23.7
Celtic Race	F.R.S.Steel	1874	263.0	39.1	23.2
Langdale	F.R.S. Iron	2047	275.0	40.1	24.2
Carnarvon Bay	F.R.S.Steel	1932	265.4	40.1	22.9
Cutty Sark	F.R.S. mixed (composite)	963	212.5	36.0	21.0
Wavertree (ex *Southgate*)	F.R.S. Iron	2170	279.0	40.2	24.4
Oweenee	Barque Steel 4m	2423	302.0	43.2	24.7
Pommern	Barque Steel 4m	2432	309.0	42.0	24.6

Built	*By*	*Owner*
Sunderland 1879	Osbourne Graham	N. Wales Shipping Co.
Sunderland 1877	Doxford	Gwynedd Shipping Co.
Sunderland 1882	Doxford	Gwynedd Shipping Co.
Sunderland 1884	Doxford	W. E. Jones
Liverpool 1877	R. & J. Evans	W. Thomas, Liverpool
Workington 1887	R. Williamson	R. Thomas & Co.
Sunderland 1891	W. Pickersgill	R. Hughes Jones & Co.
Liverpool 1885	W. H. Potter	Moel Tryvan Ship Co. (Roberts, Owen & Co.)
Glasgow Port 1894	A. Rodger & Co.	Carnarvon Bay Ship Co. (Roberts, Owen & Co.)
Dumbarton 1869	Scott & Linton	J. Willis
Southampton 1885	Oswald, Mordaunt & Co.	R. W. Leyland & Co.
Stockton 1891	Richardson, Duck & Co.	Lewis, Heron
Glasgow Port 1903	J. Read & Co.	F. Laeisz

Captain Thomas Williams, and other master mariners such as Captain William Williams of London another Black Ball line captain. Eleazer Roberts was better known in Wales for his pioneering of the Tonic Sol-Fa and his composing of the hymn 'O na bawn yn fwy tebyg i Iesu Grist yn byw'.

It is not therefore very surprising that Captain Thomas Owen and his wife, Ellen, were happy in the company of Captain Thomas Williams, having both been brought up in rural Wales, in the Calvinistic Methodist tradition, and when in Liverpool being part of the Liverpool Welsh community. The part played by Thomas Owen in the South American war as master of the *British India* brought the company to the notice of many men of integrity such as Captain James McGill. McGill was a good friend of Captain Thomas Williams as well as being very well known as Captain of the *Carnarvonshire*, and also the first captain of the *Cambrian Princess* in 1877. McGill was a shareholder in the *Cambrian Prince* and the *Cambrian Princess*. Captain McGill was managing the company more and more. Thomas Owen follows in his footsteps and Ellen Owen mentions this in her diary.

Captain Owen's predecessor on the *Cambrian Monarch* and her first master was David Hughes, a man from Caernarfon whom Thomas Williams had known from the early days. David Hughes had sailed in local schooners since he was fourteen years old, as mate on one of the Davies of Borth ships, the *Elizabeth Caroline*, and as master on the *Naval Reserve* of 1831 tons, previously owned by the famous Black Ball line and now the largest ship in Thomas Williams' fleet. There were still many large wooden sailing ships under this flag – the *British India*, 1266 tons; the *Carnarvonshire*, 1336 tons; the *Castlemaine*, 1361 tons; the *Eastern Light*, 1245 tons; the *Royal Oak* 1244 tons and the *William Levitt* 1184 tons. The ships of the late 1870s were nearly all iron ships. Thus two sister ships, the *Cambrian Princess* and the *Cambrian Prince* were on order before the *Cambrian Monarch* left the blocks.

The *Prince*, 1349 tons, was launched in 1876 and the *Princess*, exactly the same size, in 1877. Thomas Williams insured his ships in Nefyn, with the Pwllheli and Nevin Mutual Marine Insurance Company, the Provincial and Mutual Marine Insurance Company and the Provincial Shipowners Marine Mutual Protection Society. These company accounts show that each of these ships was worth £19,000 in 1877. Captain Thomas Williams and his friend from the Black Ball days, Captain William Williams were present at a meeting in the Sportsman Hotel in Caernarfon on February 28th 1878, and also at a similar meeting in the Crown Hotel in Pwllheli on St. David's Day to consider the different company accounts. At this meeting they accepted the suggestion of Captain Williams of London that a committee should be established to encourage the adoption of Lloyd's rules regarding collisions, as the insurance clubs had drawn attention to the increased cost of these during the Balkans war, and more significant to these ships, the possibility of war between Chile and Peru in South America.

A large number of losses were noted in the company accounts, and mention was made of the effect of the tidal wave on the east coast of South America in 1877, and its effect on the shipping market. Like many similar shipping companies Captain Thomas Williams was probably hoping to sell his old, wooden ships in order to finance the new, iron ships. Several North Walian companies such as Davies of Borth and William Thomas of Liverpool had ordered new ships from the yards in Sunderland and Liverpool. Just as Captain Robert Thomas foresaw problems ahead when the Borth ships were sold, Thomas Owen probably worried as to where his next ship was coming from when the *British*

India was sold. However, he was clearly at the top of the list in his company, and to reinforce his chances we see his name and the name of his ships on the list for a project close to the heart of his senior partner, namely the building of the English Presbyterian church in Cricieth. Following the names of ship brokers and ship agents from New York, Callao, Hamburg and San Francisco, on the list were also – Captain Evan Jones, *Carnarvonshire* £25.7.10; Captain Morgan, *Naval Reserve* £24.15.0; Captain William Levitt, £23.9.0; Captain McGill, *Cambrian Princess* £20; Captain Hughes, *Royal Oak* £13.2.0; Captain Evan Jones, *Eastern Light* £10.3.2; Captain Davies, *Cambrian Prince* £8.17.0; Captain Owen, *British India* £6.0.0; Captain David Hughes, *Cambrian Monarch* £5.0.0. These sums were far more than anything given by land lubbers, who gave one or two pounds each.

Lloyd's List shows that Captain David Davies left the *Cambrian Monarch* in 1879 and that Captain Thomas Owen took command in 1880, at about the time that Captain Thomas Williams died, in March 1880. Captain Owen was not at the funeral although several others were. Thomas Owen remained as Captain of the *British India* from December 1874 until the beginning of 1880. Therefore it would appear that the voyage described in Ellen Owen's journal is the second voyage made by Captain Owen as master of the *Cambrian Monarch*. Although her family claim that she sailed often with her husband there is no proof of this. We shall see in the next chapter that she shared this experience with many young Welsh women who went to sea with their husbands, although we do not know of them all. Ellen was not the first or the last but that does not decry from her diary, or the adventure.

Chapter 3

Women at Sea

February 8 The breeze is light today, but the wind is warm such as there is of it. The oranges are very good and I am very glad to have them. I hope they do not go bad. I have been crocheting since we sailed. I wash everything of my own and of Tom's. It is a pretty good place to wash. I am feeling very much at home and everyone is so nice to me. I know one thing, my underwear is spotless.

Wednesday March 15th 1882
I have not much to write about today. The ship is rolling a bit. There is very light breeze today, but it was blowing quite hard last night. I love being in heavy weather and hearing the men sing as they pull on the ropes. The poor things have to go up the masts in the night and it is so dark that they cannot see their own shadow and sometimes it is blowing really hard as well. I have a fire today. It is 145 days since we dropped our tow – the ship is rolling – I can't write anymore.

Friday March 17th 1882
It is not blowing very much today. It is rolling a bit. We are going to kill the pig this afternoon. The goat is on a shorter rope in this weather and the hens have stopped laying. I was thinking the other night when we were in that terrible weather, and it really was terrible too, how wonderful it would be to be in Cors Iago. The sailors are getting really dirty, poor things. Unimaginable to those who have not seen it.

Further anecdotes tell of the many superstitions surrounding the sea. One heavy, American tome on sea tales tells miserable stories of pigs, cats, hens, foxes, women (especially if they have nothing on their feet or are seen to be carrying buckets along the quay), lawyers or preachers all carrying the chance of bad luck, misfortune or threat of bad weather for sailors.[1] There are dozens of superstitions from as many countries to frighten would-be sailors. High on the list are those involving ships that carry women. It often seemed necessary to have someone to blame if things went wrong on the ship, someone they could call 'Jonah'. Easier still, of course, to put the blame on a woman as she would be alone in this world of men. Since then women have sailed the seas, not only as passengers but also as crew, and in Scandinavia there are quite a few ships with women officers as well as crew. From Wales women have travelled all over the world on ships, but in the last century there has been an enormous amount of movement and emigration. The 1861 census shows that women travelled in the small coasters, and I wonder who exactly was 'Ellen Jones' aged 22, domestic, at present out of situation, passenger on the sloop *Sampson* from Amlwch but anchored at Beaumaris on the night of the census, April 7th. The captain of the *Sampson* was Richard Hughes, aged 52, from Llanbadrig. The mate was Owen Jones, aged 52, from Llanbadrig also; and the able seaman, William Jones aged 14, from Amlwch. On the schooner *Sarah* anchored nearby was the captain, John Thomas, the mate, Dafydd Rowlands, two seamen from Amlwch; John Thomas aged 12 (the captain's son?) and the captain's wife, Margaret Thomas aged 34, originally from Moelfre in Anglesey. There are many sad tales of the captain's wife and family losing their lives in shipwrecks.

In those big ships that took people to a new life in America or Australia hundreds of young Welsh women tolerated several uncomfortable weeks. On August 30th 1864, the log of the *Donald McKay* shows the birth of a son to Sergeant John and Rachel Griffiths, one of eleven children born on the voyage out to Australia.[2] Most of the passengers were soldiers and their wives, but on the 8th September 1864 there was also an entry showing the death of a ten day old child, Charles Griffith. Also the following from the log of one of the Davies of Borth ships on a voyage to Melbourne:

'September 22. Wednesday. Today a young woman with everything to look forward to died. She left a grieving husband and a small baby without a mother. We committed her body to the waves in the hope of resurrection to everlasting life from the depths of the Atlantic ocean.

October 23. Today sees the ship quiet, calm and still after the death of a small baby, making a total of 27 who have died on this voyage.[3]

Hundreds of children died on these voyages, mostly from conditions that are now easily cured or avoided such as chicken pox.[4] There is no evidence of women going to sea in the Naval ships during the wars against the French at the end of the eighteenth century and the beginning of the nineteenth century. However, it is possible that some poor Welshman might have suffered the same fate as the young Scotsman born on the warship *Tremendous* on June 1st. 'Glorious 1st June, 1793, Daniel Tremendous McKenzie'.[5]

Of all the women who are recorded as having gone to sea for one reason or another, the group that enjoyed the sailing and the travel and who took the trials of that life in their stride were the captains' wives. Although tradition and superstition discouraged shipowners from allowing women on board ship, many of the wives of the captains of the larger ships spent most of their lives at sea, and many of their children were born at sea. Obviously, the shipping companies wanted to run their ships at a profit and space on board for the men was at a premium, also space for the officers and the apprentices, but the captain's cabin at the stern was the place where the business was done with the insurers or merchants in foreign ports and it was therefore laid out in some style, was large and comfortable for welcoming visitors on board. There was thus plenty of room for the captain to have his family live on board. If his wife was very sensible and did not upset the smooth running of the ship, particularly regarding the galley and the cook, and developed the art of being kind and thoughtful towards other people, other officers or to the crew, to visitors or to the owners when they came on board, then she became an asset to the company. Life on board when in foreign ports was often interesting and entertaining, but life on board for several months at sea without seeing another woman at all, with the cabin never still, wet, cold or unbearably hot, then that was another matter.

It is important to remember that coastal journeys in what was known as the home trade were very common indeed, and many captains' wives spent their honeymoon on board their husbands' ships, mostly schooners. I have mentioned in another book about Captain Henry Roberts, Moelfre, taking his wife, who was the daughter of Captain Lewis of the *Margaret Jane* and having four brothers who were well known mariners from Moelfre, on their honeymoon on the *Earl of Lathom* in 1914.[6] This ship was built in Connah's Quay by Ferguson and Laird in 1885 and they sailed from Caernarfon to Hamburg with a cargo of slates, calling at Boulogne, Ipswich, Newcastle and Pentawen before sailing home to Moelfre just before war broke out. We also hear about Captain Hugh Roberts from Porthmadog, son of the captain of the *Constance* who gave tremendous support and encouragement to the slate industry. He took his wife to sea with him on the *Evelyn*, one of the happiest ships sailing out of Porthmadog,[7] and there are photographs of her on the ship in Antwerp on their honeymoon and also later with their small daughter. Ten ships were launched in Porthmadog in the same year as the *Evelyn*, 1877, and eight in 1878. Several became quite famous such as the *Cadwaladr Jones, Frau Minna Petersen, Marianne Greaves, Martha Percival, C.E. Spooner, Edward Arthur* and *Sarah Evans*. There would have been similar hopes for the *Marie Kaestener*. She was built for Captain Richard Pritchard of Borth-y-Gest being a person who liked to have his family on board. Mrs Pritchard was on the ship together with their son when she left the Mersey bar for the short trip to Porthmadog in 1878. They were never seen again.

Another tragedy could have occurred when the brig *John Roberts*, built in Pwllheli in 1875 was forced towards the shore at Marsden near Berwick in December 1901. She had sailed from Aruba with a cargo of phosphate stone when the wind changed to an easterly, force 10. As she was going down a man threw a line to the ship and the captain's wife and all the crew were saved. The master, Captain Davies from Rhoslan, had been taken ill shortly after leaving port and by the time they reached land he was unconscious. Mrs Davies was much commended for the way in which she looked after her husband in such appalling conditions.

It is possible that Ellen Owen, although she came from North Wales, would not have heard of the loss of the *Marie Kaestner* nor earlier on, of the loss of the *Snowdonia*, whilst the *Cambrian Monarch* was en route from New South Wales to San Francisco. The *Snowdonia* was launched in the same year as the *Fleetwing*, 1874, and she was carrying a cargo of phosphate rock just like the *John Roberts* but was lost with all hands. The young woman who was to marry the skipper of the *Snowdonia* had travelled to Scotland with her brother to meet the ship only to be told of the devastating news of the loss of the ship. The wife of the captain of the *Isallt* was nearly drowned on her first night at sea when the weather changed in the Channel and they had only just left Falmouth.[8]

The voyages made by the wives of the schooner captains were short in comparison with those of the wives of the masters of the deep sea going barques. They would go to Scandinavia or Germany, to Copenhagen or Hamburg. Other than going on their honeymoon, the schooner wives might take their children away in the school holidays. The deep sea wives, however, on the fully rigged ships and the very large barques knew that they would travel the world and be on board for several months at a time, and be away from home for easily more than a year. It would be a good thing for the reader, at this point, to look over the shoulder of Ellen Owen and try to have some insight into her life on the *Cambrian Monarch* and to understand some of the experiences she would have had. It is easy in this day and age to read the diary superficially and without proper understanding of the whole picture. As we turn the pages of the log, however, we can have a better illustration of what she faced.

To begin with there was the nature of the life. From being on dry land amongst family and friends the woman condemns herself to being a prisoner in her cabin on the poop without anyone to share small talk, fears, experiences, not even able to talk about the weather. She now shares the life and weather of a mariner not that of a farmer and the centre of her life is her husband, the captain. Homesickness, seasickness, general health problems, and a feeling of isolation are all problems facing a young wife going to sea with her husband for the first time. Ellen Owen mentions her headaches ('not yet used to the sea'), and also the health of her husband such a long way from home, and hundreds of miles from a doctor. Homesickness is a great problem, mentioned many times in the diary, missing the chapel, and missing being home on a Sunday. She really misses not being near her roots. Between Ellen and her home there were hundreds and hundreds of miles of ocean, and some of the roughest seas in the world. She noted everything in her diary as she prayed for the right winds and favourable weather for the *Cambrian Monarch*, so as to bring her back to Tudweiliog as quickly as possible.

Naturally, Ellen, like all captains' wives who rounded the Horn, observed the places where many ships had been lost, but she knew she was lucky to be travelling from west to east and not the other way round. She was also lucky to be travelling in the summer months, so avoiding the terrible winds and seas encountered in the winter months. It was, of course, easy to think on these lines when in San Francisco, but according to Ellen's diary she had some pretty foul weather on this voyage. About thirty years after this another Welsh captain's wife, Catherine Thomas from Llangybi, had a dreadful voyage round the Horn on the *Criccieth Castle* sailing from the west coast of South America to Britain in 1912. Catherine and her small son were put into an open boat after the ship sank near the Falklands. A few weeks after this Catherine gave birth to a daughter whom she called Mercy Malvina Thomas.[9] She previously had another terrible experience on the well known ship *Kate Thomas*. This occurred in the channel in April 1910 when that ship was in collision with a steamer and sank without trace in a few minutes. Catherine was one of the people to survive the accident.

'All went well until about 4 o'clock in the morning when I was awakened by something banging into us. I rushed on deck and saw a light of a steamer sheering off. I rushed back to get some clothes and then went on the poop where I saw the captain and his wife, the chief officer and his wife and the third officer. The captain's wife shouted to the tug for help and the chief officer's wife was very calm and collected. She was quite a young woman... the *Kate Thomas* gradually keeled over. We were all hanging on for about eight minutes until she gave one final plunge. I got a lifebuoy and sprang clear to try to save myself from being sucked down. Two or three huge waves enveloped me and when I looked round there was nothing but a mass of foam and the *Kate Thomas* had gone'.[10]

In the book *Meistri'r Moroedd* I was able to re-read one of the best known stories from the windjammer world of the 19th century, namely the attempted saving of the crew of the *Cambrian Chieftain* by the sailing ship *Dee* during a dreadful storm in the Pacific ocean in 1894. Captain Hugh Thomas' wife and two children were saved from the ship by one of the lifeboats from the *Dee*. The lifeboat crew lost their lives when returning to the *Cambrian Chieftain* to rescue the remainder of the crew.[11]

Shipwreck was not the only test that young women who went to sea with their husbands faced. Many children were born on board ship mostly when they were many hundreds of miles from land or port. One of the families who travelled the world at this time was that of Captain Owen Jones and his wife, Mary, both from Cricieth. Ellen Jones, their daughter, was born in Pisco, Peru, on July 1st 1877, and her brother on 23rd December 1879, near Callao, where their father's ship, the *Havelock*, was waiting, with many others, for a cargo of guano.[12] Captain William Griffith and his wife had a daughter who was born within sight of San Francisco after the ship had been thrown on to her head as they rounded the Horn. They called the child Francisco Griffith. J. Ifor Davies writes in his book, *Growing Up Among Sailors* how his father heard, on reaching Valparaiso, that the captain of the *Kirkcudbrightshire* had a new son and that he was to be called Valpo Roberts. Ifor Davies' book tells of the life he and his sister led in Nefyn and on the *Gwydyr Castle* with their parents, Captain William Davies and Mrs Davies. Basil Lubbock praises Captain Roberts of the *Kirkcudbrightshire* in *The Last of the Windjammers*. He was master of that ship from 1903 to 1922.

As it happens there is a reference to the *Kirkcudbrightshire* in a diary that has just come to light,[13] that of Ellen, the wife of Captain Griffith Jones who was master of two of the ships owned by Captain Thomas Owen, the *Langdale* (1905 to 1912) and the *Grenada* (1912 to 1916). We now digress to the business side of the marine world of that time. Ellen Griffith, the daughter of Penlan Bach, Pwllheli, married Griffith Jones, the son of Captain Griffith Jones, *Pegasus*, Nefyn at St. David's church, Liverpool on January 28th 1904. The wedding was arranged, and many guests invited, but the wind changed direction and the wedding had to be brought forward by two hours so that the *Langdale* could set sail for Hongay, China. (*Only the best man, Captain Kingham, the first mate, and the bridesmaid, Ellen's sister, Mary, were present.*) Captain Jones returned in May and in July 1905 his wife started to accompany him on his voyages, this time from Antwerp to San Francisco. There is a beautiful painting of the *Langdale* done by John Henry Mohrmann showing her under full sail and with the captain and his wife on the poop, which hangs on the wall of their grandaughter's home even today. Over the following years

John and Moraned on board Langdale.
Moraned was born on the ship

Ellen Jones rounded the Horn at least six times, and the children accompanied their parents. John, the elder, was born in Penlan Bach, Pwllheli, but joined the ship with his mother at the age of six weeks. He lived on the *Langdale* until he was six years old, at which time he had to go to school. He remembers his sister being born on the *Langdale* in January 1909, in the North Atlantic. She was given the name Moraned. Captain and Mrs Jones were hoping to reach Europe sooner but they were becalmed off the Azores. After noting in her diary that they had crossed the equator on January 6th 1909, 68 days after leaving Caleta Colosa, she then wrote 'Baby born in North Atlantic, 37° 42'N 33°W, 5a.m.'

Captain Jones, who delivered the baby, went up on to the poop and said 'Gentlemen we have another passenger'. Moraned was weaned on ship biscuits and tinned evaporated milk, and had happy memories of sleeping in a hammock, far more practical than any cot. The birth was registered in Hamburg from whence the *Langdale* sailed on her next, aforementioned, voyage with John and Moraned on board with their parents.

To the north of the equator and in the doldrums they sighted the *Kirkcudbrightshire* and Captain Jones knew that Captain Roberts had his family on board. The signal flags were soon out inviting the Roberts' to tea on the *Langdale*.

The next day Captain Jones and his wife were invited back to the *Kirkcudbrightshire* and Ellen Jones notes in her diary how glad she was to see and to speak with another woman. *(In later years my mother was heard by me to say to my grandmother, 'I don't know how you could go to tea with the Roberts' and leave me in my cot on the* Langdale. *What if the wind had returned?' My grandmother replied that 'It was not quite as bad as that, Moraned. Your Father and Captain Roberts understood these things. We were all quite safe.' Nothing ruffled my grandmother.)*

One of the family treasures from Captain and Mrs Jones is the collection of postcards in the possession of Captain John Griffith Jones, the son who was on the *Langdale*, and his niece, Elinor Ellis, their grandaughter. They were sent to John from all parts of the world by his father, the captain, after John had left the ship to start school in Pwllheli, and also cards to Moraned after she and her mother came ashore for her schooling, and later because of the first world war. The cards sent to John are almost without exception those of some of the large sailing ships that he saw when he was at sea with his father, or cards of ships belonging to his father's friends, with messages on the back e.g. 'Here is a photo of the *Oweenee* to put in your album', or 'Uncle Wil (Captain William Griffith, Captain Jones brother-in-law, friend, and himself master of the *Carnarvon Bay*) has asked for a picture of the *Howard D. Troop*, for you in Dublin, and yesterday I got it from the captain'. After Moraned left the ship the longing for his family was clear, as shown in the card from New York in 1915. 'Daddy is really missing his little girl who is in Pwllheli'. We see the same sentiments in the cards sent by Captain Owen Barlow Pritchard to his little daughter, Myfi, showing his homesickness for Llanllyfni, and in the letters sent by Captain Robert Thomas of Llandwrog to his children. It is difficult to know which is the harder situation, missing the family after they have been on the ship for some time, like most captains, or not being allowed to take them in the first place like the masters of the Davies of Borth company. There is plenty of evidence that this company lost several good masters because of the rule, in particular Captain William Williams of Rhiw and Captain Thomas Williams of Caernarfon.

Melbourne House, Burnt Ash Hill, Lee and other, later, homes in Blackheath and Lewisham were full of treasures that Mrs William Williams had brought home from abroad. She was the wife of the boy from Rhiw who became captain and owner of some of the largest sailing ships in the world. He had left the company of Richard Davies, Treborth, because they would not allow the wives to sail. In the memoirs of one of her daughters in East Orange, New Jersey, half a century later, this lady is described as beautiful, with a heavy gold collar from Australia round her neck, and surrounded by ebony furniture and wonderful pictures from China, plus elegant lace and craftwork from all over the world.[14]

It is sad to have to write about young wives who died when travelling with their husbands. This happened to Captain Barlow Pritchard after his successful voyage in the ship *Glenesslin* from Portland, Oregon to East Africa at the beginning of the century. The late Commodore Gerald N. Jones was an apprentice on the *Glenesslin* and his articles in *Sea Breezes* and the *Cymro* described the anguish of the crew when the captain's young wife was taken ashore to the hospital in Laurenco Marques, Mozambique. She died and was buried in the small cemetery above the town. Commodore Jones records how kind Mrs Pritchard was to the apprentices, and to the crew on the ship, and showed a photograph of her on the poop with her husband. Later, Gerald Jones who became a high ranking officer in the navy and, during the second world war, commodore of the convoys and captain of one of Cunard's larger ships, said he had never forgotten that lonely grave in Mozambique. Another wife who died at sea, although a lot nearer home, was Mary Ann Meredith of the ship *Dominion*. She died within sight of Ireland on the way home from San Francisco. The words 'Ar fôr tymhestlog teithio 'rwyf' are on her memorial stone in Llandegfan churchyard.[15] Despite having travelled the world, many wives requested burial at home in Wales. An example of this is demonstrated in a letter from the captain of the *Forest King*, one of the sailing ships belonging to Captain William Humphrey Owen, Rhuddgaer, Anglesey. It was written in May 1868, in English, being the language in which all owners and captains corresponded, despite the fact that they all spoke and wrote Welsh.

Ship *Forest King*
Callao, 20 May 1868

Dear Sir,

No doubt you will think it strange being so long without hearing from me but I hope when you have heard of my sickness and all my troubles you will excuse me. My poor wife died of dysentry on 26 April after a month of illness. I have her remains on board being her last wish that I should have her buried at home. For 10 days after her death I was not out of bed labouring under a heavy fever and had but a very narrow escape of following her.

After I wrote cash to you I had bought time at 30$ today. We left Chincha on Wednesday 13, save 25 days, arrived here on Friday morning. On that day I went ashore but soon had to return finding myself sick. I had shipped my crew and had everything ready to sail next day except settling with O'Connor. I had to send for a Doctor who said as soon as he saw me I had the Yellow

Fever. I was put in a hot mustard bath and had a severe course of medicine. On Monday I took a turn for the better. Today I am out of bed thanks to the Almighty, but very weak and I intend to sail this afternoon ... the Yellow Fever is still very bad here, in fact nearly all the foreigners in Callao are dead. It is now very bad in Lima, dying at the rate of 300 a day there.[16]

Despite the dangers women from all over the world continued to go to sea with their husbands. Dr. Jurgen Mayer's book *Hamburg's Segelshiffe 1795–1945*, has many excellent photographs of German women who sailed the world e.g. Kapitan Detlef Thedeus, his wife and crew of the *Maipo* from Hamburg; Kapitan Johannes Stehr, his wife and crew of the *Bretrand* in Itzehoe; Kapitan Julius Tadsen and his family on the *Wandsbek II* in San Francisco. Captain John P. Parker in his detailed study *Cape Breton Ships and Men* mentions several women who sail with their husbands. Captain John Lowray took his family with him and they sailed the Atlantic in the same year as Ellen Owen's diary was written. Captain C. M. Burchall from Sydney, Cape Breton sailed round the world on the *Oweenee* with his wife and daughter, the ship being very well known to Welsh seafarers, particularly when under the command of Captain Robert Jones of Amlwch.[17]

Captain Parker claimed that Nellie, Captain Burchell's daughter, had sailed on the *Oweenee* from birth until the age of eleven, being taught by her mother in preparation for going to school. Nellie remembers her mother treating the hands of several of the crew after a cargo of iron shifted during a voyage from Middlesborough to Kobe in Japan in 1897, and also of her being absolutely adamant that neither she nor her dog would venture beyond the poop. Another memory was of the ship's cook, a man from China, going off his head and having to be incarcerated for his own sake and that of everyone on the ship. There are more tales of the *Oweenee* later on after she was bought by Captain Thomas Owen & Co., Tudweiliog. Basil Lubbock has quite a bit to say about captains' wives in his book *The Last of the Windjammers*. We should note that the wife of one of the best known sea captains and owners, the Norwegian Captain Gustaf Erikson, began her married life by sailing from Swansea on the *Albania* in 1906. This tale is told in *The Last of the Tall Ships* by George Kahre.

Thus Ellen Owen was not doing anything unusual by the standards of the maritime communities by sailing on the *Cambrian Monarch* with her husband. In all fairness to Captain Owen it was far healthier to travel to Australia and San Francisco than to the nitrate and guano ports of South West America. She therefore avoided the medical conditions that could be picked up in those ports. However no-one could predict what would happen at sea, regardless of the weather. The wife of the captain of the *Cambrian King* had an appalling voyage in March 1897 when 20 ships close to them were wrecked. The *Cambrian King* was thrown on her beam ends, causing the cargo to shift. With the ship on her side, salt water swished through the captain's cabin and his wife had to hold the baby above her head as the men pulled the two of them out about 10 minutes after the ship capsized. No wonder all and sundry talked of the wife on the *King* and her courage in waiting for help when she had her baby with her. Her husband said 'I cannot say too much for the splendid bravery she showed during the hurricane. At one time she was up to her armpits in water with the ship working heavily and holding her little daughter above her head. We were forced to drag them out through the stateroom sky light, the door being under water and jammed.' A few months after she sailed for Australia in the

Monarch in 1881 Ellen Owen also experienced a cabin full of water, ruining her furniture and her clothes, not to mention family photographs and personal possessions. It is time for me to join her on the *Cambrian Monarch*.

Chapter 4

The Diary

The *Cambrian Monarch* sailed from Newport, Monmouthshire on May 12th 1881 reaching Sydney, New South Wales, on August 12th.[1] We do not, however, have any letters or diary entries for this part of the voyage other than one for the second day out of San Francisco where she notes that, 'We have had a better start from here than either from Newport or Sydney.' It is most likely that it was on the first half of this voyage that they had the terrible weather that caused so much damage in their cabin. Remembering that the diary was being written for her sister, it may be that she did not want to frighten Sarah unnecessarily by giving unpleasant details, especially as she was intending to make several more voyages. Whatever the reason it was certainly on this voyage in 1881/82 that the excessive damage occurred, as a case came up before the magistrates in the London Police Court on the 2nd August 1882 from Captain Thomas Owen, 143 East India Dock Road, Poplar, Middlesex for renewal of his captain's ticket. Captain Owen of the ship *Cambrian Monarch* testified that he had passed captain in February 1873 and that since then he had sailed on the *British India* and the *Cambrian Monarch*, but that he now needed a renewal of his ticket due to damage that was done on the voyage from San Francisco to Sydney, 'By salt water on last voyage, the sea having broken in through the skylight and nearly half filled the cabin'. His captain's ticket was renewed on August 4th, 1882.[2]

There is no definite proof as to whether this is the only really long voyage that Ellen made, but she certainly travelled to many European ports to meet her husband on his return from deep sea trips. The lovely photograph of her with her husband taken by Otto Joop in Hamburgh was probably taken in the early days of their marriage i.e. between 1876 and 1880. This is pure surmise as there is no date on the picture. The other photograph was probably taken when he was captain of the *British India* soon after he was commended for his action in avoiding the siege in Mexilliones. He is wearing a silk hat, thus showing the extrovert side of his nature. We can imagine how proud Ellen was of her good looking husband when she left Tyddyn Sander for Newport and the trip to Australia.

From May 1881 to August 1882, never mind about any other time, the *Cambrian Monarch* was Ellen's home and it is well described in the diary. As you look from the stern to the bow, the captain's cabin would be on the right on the starboard side. The first mate also had a cabin in this part of the ship, on the left, the port side. The main cabin, too, was here, a large living room where the meals were served. These were very spacious, comfortable rooms, especially when compared with the crew's quarters.[3] In earlier days Captain Owen had a carpenter's workshop and he would appreciate the mahogany or teak panelling in these large cabins. Ellen, too, was glad of something to do such as choose pictures and furnishings for the cabin. Of course, she would have to be careful not to tread on the steward's toes as he was responsible for the 'housework' here, including the meals. One can get a good picture of how these ships were run by the specifications from the builder; the steward's store, the galley store, the ship's carpenter's store, the sailmaker's store. Sometimes there was a list of things belonging to the master as opposed to those belonging to the ship. For example, when Roberts, Owen and Co. bought the *Langdale* from the Dale line in 1904, there was a list amongst the Kellocks' (the brokers)[4] papers of Captain Hunter's personal possessions: piano with piano stool; gramaphone;

2 armchairs and 4 deck chairs; 2 bikes; 1 footbath; mattresses, nightdresses, bedding; 1 square mirror; clothes of every type belonging to the captain and his wife; 1 silver teaset; 1 china teaset; jugs; kettles; oil lamps, bookshelves, pencil boxes; one gun in guncase; 1 spyglass; 2 chronometers; 2 sextants; charts and seafaring papers; pictures; books; clothes chests and chart chests; many other things and a quantity of nick-nacks. These all belonged to the captain and his wife as opposed to the ship. Changing ship is, to them, like moving house. *(Taid took over from Captain Hunter in 1904).*

When Ellen Owen started her diary she had been away from home for nine months and had had enough of life on board ship. She was, after all, a farmer's daughter and was writing to her sister in Pwllcwd and later in Tyddyn Sander. Small wonder then that Ellen took her home world with her – the animals on the ship, washing clothes, knitting, sewing, the chapel, and she became homesick for the fields and the smell of the earth. The *Cambrian Monarch* reached San Francisco from Sydney, after eleven weeks at sea, on the 9th December 1881.[5] Thus they were in San Francisco over Christmas and until February 4th 1882 when they sailed out of that perfect bay, having bought several pieces of furniture for their home in Tudweiliog. These were destined for the house that they intended to have built on the piece of land knows as Cors Iago, land they had been negotiating for over some time. There is very little mention of this in the diary. The bedroom furniture and the chairs in the front parlour at Minafon were known by the family as 'The San Francisco furniture'. This was Ellen's home until the 1930's.

There is no date or place on the photograph of Ellen taken with the crew and with her husband at her side,[6] but it was probably San Francisco or Sydney from the 1882/3 voyage on the *Cambrian Monarch*. Although the entire crew are not present it seems that the more important people are: the officers, the craftsmen, the apprentices and the 'afterguard'. Unfortunately, I do not have the articles or the crew agreements lists for this voyage. They are not with the Gwynedd Archives, nor at Greenwich. The young apprentices are to be seen sitting at the feet of the captain's wife, although none of them, nor the people behind her, are taking any notice of her or the camera. It looks as though some animal has moved from between the knees of the middle apprentice and he, himself, moved just as the photo was being taken. Next to the very young apprentice on the right, maybe he is the cabin boy, there is a hen coop, and on the knee of the man by the rigging there is the body of a much larger bird. We know that Thomas Owen's brother in law was on this voyage (married to his sister, Ann), and he is most likely to be the man with the soft hat contrasting with the silk topped hat of the captain standing by the main mast. The mate is probably the man sitting on the extreme left with his feet on the hatch, and the sailmaker is on the right with a tool in the right hand. Whoever all these people are they are Ellen's companions for the voyage and made up of Welsh, English, Russian/Finns (as the Scandinavians were often called), a truly international crew as was common on these large sea going sailers at that time.

This photo is similar to hundreds of others taken in foreign ports but is of more interest than most because of the variety of people in it. The traditional dress of ship's masters at that time was the tall, silk hat and the dickey bow. Captain Owen was very conscious of his position and of that of his wife who is well dressed as befitted a captain's wife of that era.[7] She looks up to her husband in all things as was expected in the age of Queen Victoria.

One of Ellen's greatest friends at home in Llŷn was Thomas's brother in law, Richard Davies, Weirglodd Fawr.[8]

He is well remembered in the area to this day as a very able man, a craftsman and a gentleman in the true sense of the word. After leaving the sea he became the supporter of many projects in Tudweiliog including teaching in the Sunday school, and a very good friend to Thomas and Ellen Owen. It was he who sent copies of the sermons of John Jones, Talsarnau, for her to read on her voyage home, and she felt much in his debt. This religious background to the diary is, maybe, difficult for today's reader to appreciate but it was part of the middle class background of the day and Ellen was typically naive, devout, unassuming and sincere. Captain Thomas Owen and Richard Davies, like Ellen, played an important part in, and were a good example of, Welsh life in the late nineteenth century.[9]

The log we have is of the voyage and, therefore, there is no mention of the time spent in San Francisco over Christmas 1881. It is a pity that we could not find the letters she sent home in order to compare them with those written by Catherine Bruce Thomas twenty years later, during the time that she was in San Francisco when her father, Captain Robert Thomas of the *Afon Alaw*, was so ill. Brucey's description of San Francisco Bay, the beautiful ships, the women's clothes, life in the cafes, the beautiful weather and the flowers on the route to the Cypress Lawns cemetery made a very memorable picture. Her description of the view on the day of her father's burial, and the long line of seamen following the cortege, many of whom were Welsh, was vivid. 'What a comfort it was to see all the rugged brown faces of the men, most all in shabby blue suits but each with a black tie, and steady and respectful'.[10] There were so many large sailing ships with Welshmen as captains in the second half of the nineteenth century that it was not surprising to see so many compatriots at Captain Robert's funeral.

One of the best books on that era is by the Padre to the

Seamen's Institute, the mission building in Steuart Street in the dockland area of San Francisco; *British Merchant Seamen in San Francisco* by the Reverend James Fell. Fell was a courageous man taking on the crimps such as 'Shanghai Kelly', 'Chicken Divine', and others who ruined the lives of many a seaman. 'Calico Jim', 'Three Fingered Daly' and 'Scabby Joe' were all people who enticed naive mariners with promise of a good time, got them thoroughly drunk, took their money and then sold them to second rate ships' mates who could not find crews. The victim would wake up on a ship going he knew not where and penniless. After describing the problems of the port Fell goes on to describe the tale of a young North Walian as an example of his work with people of every nationality, when the Seamen's Institute would take care of a man's money whilst he was in port. This young man came straight from his ship and asked the Institute if they would look after £20 of his wages, and he intended to lodge there until he could get another ship, probably about a month. Fell soon found that this lad was not only a popular fellow but he also had a strong Christian faith. 'It is not easy for a sailor paid off in San Francisco, far from home, practically a stranger, to live as he did'. Eventually he got a berth on a ship sailing north to load timber for Britain and he asked Fell to send the rest of his pay, about £16, home to his father in Wales. On the new ship the boy met a relative of his, a middle aged man who was rather a drunkard. The boy persuaded the man to come with him that evening to the Institute, and Fell talked with the two of them at some length. About 4p.m. the next day Fell noticed that the flag of the young man's ship was flying at half mast. The young Welshman was high up working on the yards when he slipped and fell to his death. He was buried in San Francisco at a time when Thomas and Ellen Owen were there with the *Cambrian Monarch* and they may well have been at the service.[11]

'On the rough hillside near the Cliff House overlooking the Golden Gate, the place where most seamen from British ships find their last resting place, there might have been seen a gathering of some thirty or forty Welsh sailors, including several captains, assembled to see their young countryman laid beneath the sod. It was a wild and wet morning about 8:30a.m. and a truly touching scene it was as the solemn words of the British Service were read over him who had been so suddenly taken away. Especially sad was it to witness the great emotion of the old sailor, his relation. One thought must ever remain with him, perhaps to his great benefit, that the last act of the young man's life on earth was to try and do him good.' A few hours later the ship passed out through the Golden Gate, away into the waters of the wide Pacific and we can well believe that every eye glanced up to the hillside where the young man lay, and every mind had a thought for him whose spirit had winged its way on another voyage, a long voyage, with an innumerable company... who, like our brave sailor, had 'fought the good fight and kept the faith'.

Otherwise, Ellen may only have heard the story as she sailed past the Golden Gate to the Pacific ocean in February 1882. The tugs and pilot would have been left behind and the first and second mates would have been busy with the new crew, arranging watches and getting some teamwork together, a mixture of Scandinavians and Welsh. We hear very little of the running of the ship from Ellen. Just as the ship's log starts with the state of the weather and the wind force, so does each day of Ellen's diary, and ends with the miles covered, knowing that her husband will let her know this every day. We observe her interest in the sailors and her compassion for them in the bad weather. She talks about the accidents they suffer and the fact that her husband and the mate see to their medical needs, acting as doctor when the need arises. 'Tom has been a good doctor today'.[12] Naturally, Ellen's writing is somewhat dependent on the weather, but the important thing is to keep going whatever the weather, hot or cold, the ship rolling or not, 'I can hardly stand up today as the ship is rolling so much. I am busy trying to cover the sofa and the lockers. We covered 200 miles yesterday. It is very comforting to see another ship, breaking the loneliness of the life at sea for a woman. The ship that we saw yesterday is with us again today. There is a wife on board. They hope to go to Queenstown for orders as long as the wind is favourable'. Ellen is homesick, especially on Sundays. 'I often think about going to Penllech chapel or to Tudweiliog. But we also have very enjoyable Sundays'. Despite Thomas Owen playing his concertina and all the reading that was done, the washing of clothes and the knitting, by May the lack of wind and the consequent becalming coming immediately after the ship covering so much distance so quickly, sees Ellen sitting on the poop thinking of the colours of the spring in Llŷn and wishing she could feel the slightest breeze. The oranges, the goat and the hens were all a consolation to her and she knitted socks for the men whose wages were £2.10 a month. So far she is very happy on the ship, accepting the terms of the sea.

As we look over Ellen's shoulder writing the diary it is important to remember that it is written for her sister, Sarah, back home in Tyddyn Sander and we are honoured to travel with her from San Francisco to Queenstown (now Cobh, S Ireland). Ellen was not one to complain, 'It is 12 weeks since we sailed. We have had a good passage and thank God for that. He has been a good Lord to us on this passage keeping us safe in all weathers and in the face of all dangers.' These were not empty words on Ellen's part. She had great faith in the Almighty and she was well aware of the dangers of the sea. To remind the reader these are a few of the casualties mentioned in the maritime press:

Cambrian Duchess: Lost in a storm near Falklands, April 1880.
Belle of Arvon: Co. R. Thomas, Cricieth. Lost near the Galapagos Islands. Peru. Aug. 1899.
British Commerce: Co. W. Thomas, Liverpool. Lost in a collision in the Channel. 1883.
British Empire: Co. Davies, Porth Aethwy. On fire Indian Ocean. 1883.
Bryn Gwyn: Co. David Morgan, Dwyran. Lost in Singapore. 1887.
Cambrian Chieftain: Lost in a beam sea. Southern Ocean. 1894.
Cambrian Hills: Sank near the Scillies. 1905.
Cambrian King: Lost on voyage to Capetown from Newcastle with cargo of coal.
Cambrian Prince: Sank in the North sea. March 1903.
Cambrian Princess: Sank following a collision in the Channel. 1902.
Cape Wrath: Co. W. Thomas, Liverpool. Lost with all hands on voyage from Callao to Astoria. November 1900.
Caradoc: Lost on voyage to Kobe. Japan. Sept. 1898.
Carnedd Llewellyn: Co. R. Hughes-Jones, Liverpool. Lost near Cape Horn. 1908.
County of Carnarvon: Lost near New Zealand. July 1899.
County of Denbigh: Lost on voyage from Astoria to Britain. 1880.
Eastern Light: Lost on voyage from Penseacola to Cardiff (cargo: wood). July 1899.

These are only a few examples from the lists of casualties. Therefore please remember when you read this diary that Ellen's voyage emulates the voyages of generations of Welsh mariners and their families who travelled thousands of miles from their homes in Wales. The thing that is special about this diary is that Ellen has returned with the story, and that it is written in Welsh by a Welsh woman about a voyage 'round the Horn'. It is very easy to talk about going 'round the Horn' these days. It was a completely different matter to travel home on a sailing ship from San Francisco in the eighteenth and nineteenth centuries.

The Diary

Ship *Cambrian Monarch*
San Francisco
California
4 February 1882

I have decided to keep a bit of a log on this occasion. Here we are setting sail for England with little hope of reaching our destination safely. The steamer and the pilot have left us. I have a bit of a headache. I am not yet used to the sea. I think I shall go to bed early tonight, although I am not sick either.

5 February. Sunday
We have had a good start to this voyage. It is the first Sunday of the journey. We have had a much better start than from Newport last May[13] or from Sydney in Sept.[14] I hope this lovely, light wind continues for a spell. We are clear of the channel and I feel quite well today. The Great Lord is good

to us. Every Sunday I think about how I used to go to Penllech Chapel and to Tudweiliog. But we spend some very happy Sundays. (160 miles).

February 6. Monday
We have done four hundred miles since the tow and the wind is still favourable. Let us hope it carries on like this until we pick up the 'Trades'. The good Lord is smiling on us. (221m)

7 February
Another day dawns and thank God for it. The wind is still in our favour with a lovely breeze. (124m)

February 8th
The breeze is lighter today but the wind is still favourable, such as there is of it. The oranges are very good. I am glad that we have so many of them as long as they do not go bad. I have been crocheting since we sailed. I shall do my own washing, and Tom's as well. It is quite a nice place to wash. I feel thoroughly at home and everyone is so pleasant to me. I know one thing: all my underwear is spotless. (122m)

February 9th
The weather is much the same again today, slightly slow. I have washed all morning. I had not done so for a bit. I have made several things since we left. I have made socks and done some sewing. Tom was not very well when we left 'Frisco. He is much better since we sailed. I was afraid he would get worse after leaving. The opposite has occurred thank the Lord. I have been in very good health. (73m)

February 10th 1882. Friday
The weather is again the same, pretty slow. We have not travelled very far either yesterday or today. I hope it is not like this much longer. I have hemmed 10 napkins just for us. (45m)

February 11 1882. Saturday
Here we are having picked up the 'Trades' at last. We are moving quite quickly today. We have been moving forward since a week today namely the day that we really sailed well. I hope it continues. Tom thinks we will make good time. (95m)

Sunday. February 12th 1882
We have a lovely warm wind today and we are 'steaming' ahead, and very comfortably. But the ship is rolling. This is the second Sabbath of the voyage and Richard Davies[15] has lent me the book of sermons by John Jones, Talsarnau, and I am really enjoying them. It is a very large book and I read it to my husband and he pontificates on the odd verse, like a sermon. It is fun. Tom has a concertina and he plays the old tunes on it. (140)

Monday. February 13th 1882
We have a fair wind today and are moving well. I can't write as the ship is shaking. (120m)

Tuesday. February 14th 1882
The weather is the same again and again I cannot write as the ship is pitching. (190m)[16]

Wednesday. February 15th 1882
We have the same weather, a nice warm wind, and thank God for it. He is good with his providence. I can't write. You

can see by my writing that the ship is rolling. We have had a fair wind since we sailed. The weather is getting very warm. We are nearing the 'line', namely the centre of the world.[17] When we left 'Frisco I had a fire in the cabin and 2 thick, heavy blankets on the bed, the ones from home, and we were sleeping in the feather mattress. Now we have taken the feather mattress off and are sleeping with practically nothing on at all, with the windows open, and we are still perspiring like mad, soaked. It is eleven days since we sailed. And, yes, the change is very sudden, the water is hot. I don't need to warm the water to wash. The washing will not be great. I have not had a bath yet. I will do soon. (220m)

Thursday. 16th February 1882
Another new day. The time is passing quickly from day to day. We have a warm, strong wind again today, and thank goodness for it. We are moving ahead very quickly. I have been washing lots of clothes today. I will be feeling much better after doing the washing. I shall have some appetite for my dinner. The oranges are wonderful in this hot weather. I am so glad to have plenty of them on such a long passage as this. (210m).

Friday. February 17th 1882
The wind is lighter today. It is very hot and I am nearly melting in these clothes, although I have hardly anything on. I am very glad that we have the goat with us. It is important in this weather. (124m)

Saturday. 18th February 1882
We have a good breeze today. We are moving on very well. But the sun is so hot. It gets hotter every day, and that is how it will be for some time. There is nothing else to be expected for some spell, however. We are in the sort of weather that

they, the sailors call the doldrums,[18] sometimes calm and sometimes puffs of wind and heavy rain, heavier than you would ever see in England, and sometimes with next to no wind it is very difficult weather to tolerate. We were held up in it for ages on the way from Sydney to 'Frisco. But I don't think we shall be held up so long this time. We have had very good weather taking us onwards. Thank goodness for this. Tom has never had such a good start, he says. We are between the two trades, the north and south trades, a short way from the line. It is a fortnight since we sailed, and we have come this far nine days quicker than last time. I hope we get the same again. A warm wind is very comfortable. My health is very good. (30m.)

Sunday. 19th February 1882
Again we have a new Sabbath. Thank the Lord for it. We lose much privilege being away like this from holy services. I miss it dreadfully on occasions, thinking how wonderful it would be to go to chapel on Sunday. The poor sailors are losing so much. I don't think anyone who listens to a sermon every Sunday can appreciate it like these sailors would. We think we are picking up the other 'trade', the South trade. (60m)

Monday. 20th February 1882
We have got the 'trade' now. We are very near the line today. It will be tomorrow if we are alive and well. It is Pancake Tuesday tomorrow and we make pancakes just the same even though we are at sea. It is a great pleasure to write a little like this every day. I am glad I thought of doing it. I am thinking of getting on with some washing now. I have been mending socks. It was heavy rain this morning. It looks the same this afternoon. It's squally. (90m)

Tuesday. February 21 1882
Pancake Tuesday. We are crossing the line and we have very strong currents. We are travelling forward very quickly. We are really moving. We have covered a quarter of our journey home. We have pancakes today to celebrate Pancake Tuesday, and also crossing the line. We have come so quickly, thank the Lord. I can hardly write as the ship is moving fast (very?). She is rolling quite a bit. Difficult to write. (180m.)

Wednesday. 22 February 1882
We have a good breeze today. We are travelling along like a steamer. There is an auction here today.[19] I do not have much to spare from the slop chest.[20] It starts at half past one after we have had our dinner. (170)

Thursday. February 23 1882
It is really hot today. But it will be cold again in another fortnight, if we are alive and well. We are now further from the line each day. We had an enjoyable auction yesterday. The things I sent went very well. I could sell much more if I had made more. I sold five pairs of stockings. I have sold pounds worth of stockings altogether and they wanted even more, if I had made more to sell. But I will sell more before I get home, if I live to do so. I have another 15 pairs, I have knitted lots on the passage out; I made 7 pairs of socks and got 4 shillings a pair for some of those yesterday. (130m)

Friday. 24 February 1882
It is terribly hot today. I am soaked with sweat, and I have next to nothing on. The oranges are wonderful in this weather. (125m)

Saturday. 25th February 1882
It is three weeks since we sailed from 'Frisco. We have come along very well so far. A good breeze today. Despite that it is very easy, but very hot; yesterday and today are hotter than it has been on this voyage. The hot weather will continue. I can't eat and am perspiring a lot. We will be in cold weather again soon and from that into hot weather again and will go home with 'something'. (170m)

Sunday. 26th February
Yet another new Sabbath. We have a strong breeze of fair wind today. It is very hot. The sun is right over our heads. This hot weather is making me ill and I can't eat, and am soaked with sweat. We will not be in this heat for much longer. We will be in cold weather when we round the Cape Horn. We have had a very good passage so far, thank the good Lord for that. It is now a quarter to two in the afternoon and with you it is a quarter past ten at night. You are eight and a half hours ahead of us now. (180m)

Monday. 27th February 1882
The sun is unbearably hot today. I have no stomach for anything and everyone here is the same. (193m)

Tuesday. February 28th 1882
The last day of February. I have nothing to say today except that the weather is the same and we are all coping well in these distressing conditions. (180m)

Wednesday. March 1st 1882
Same weather again. Still very hot indeed. Moving along very well. We have not had any unfavourable winds since we left, through some mercy. We should be so grateful for this mercy, in comparison with some. (140m)

Thursday. March 2nd 1882
We have the same weather today. I think there is some thunder around. My blood is boiling. Until now I have put the miles we have travelled in red ink across the log, but from now on I shall write them in black ink. Today we have come 130miles.

Friday. 3rd March 1882
Another new day. We had some heavy squalls last night. It is thundery weather just now. We are near islands and there is always weather like this around them. Elizabeth and Pitcairn[21] islands, we shall pass them tonight. We are not very close to them. I don't expect we shall see them if the wind stays as it is. There is sometimes a very large moon these nights. 120 miles since yesterday.

March 4th. Saturday. 1882
We sailed 4 weeks today. We have covered a good bit of this long passage we have to make to come home. We have covered 140 miles.

Sunday. March 5th 1882
The Sabbath again. Our time is counted like this from Sabbath to Sabbath. I should love to live nearer to home. I really miss not going to chapel on the Sabbath. 150 miles today.

Monday. March 6th 1882
Now we are losing the trades. The weather is getting colder and we cannot expect anything else. We are approaching Cape Horn and it is always cold there. We have come 92 miles since yesterday.

Tuesday. March 7th 1882
I have no will to write today. We are all alive and well. That is an honour in itself, when we are so far from home. The hot weather took its toll of me but it is getting colder. 95 miles since yesterday.

Wednesday. 8 March 1882
We have an easy wind. We have not moved very far since yesterday. 92 miles. It is a lovely day today. Not too hot. I have been washing all morning and I have done a good bit of knitting. The oranges are keeping well and they are very good. The hens are laying quite well, but they will stop doing so before long until we have rounded the Horn. I don't expect that I shall be able to write in the heavy weather. It sometimes rolls too much to write.

Thursday. 9 March
We are alive and well again today through His grace. Thank God for looking after us day and night. The weather has become much colder by now. The old Horn will be showing its teeth quite soon. The albatrosses are starting to come and meet us showing that we are coming into rough weather. I feel much better since the weather has cooled. Tom is properly better by now. 170 miles since midday yesterday.

Friday. 10 March 1882
It is getting much colder every day. We have a good strong wind. We have only seen one ship since we sailed from 'Frisco; we have accompanied each other for about a fortnight. We sometimes don't see each other for a couple of days, and then see each other all the time for several days. We are a long way from each other. The ship is called the *Golden Gate*. 185m since yesterday.[22]

Saturday 11 March 1882
It is a lovely day today. It is 5 weeks since we sailed and we have been very lucky with the voyage so far. Let's hope the second half is as good. We had a pretty awful passage from Sydney to 'Frisco. The little goat is as fat as a cow. One of the sailors is making us a mat.[23] We think it would be a good idea to have three so that we can have one at home. We have come 180 miles today.

Sunday. March 12th 1882
It is a lovely Sabbath today. We have a favourable, comfortable wind that carries us forward brilliantly. The Lord is very good to us although we do not deserve this grace. I have been reading the sermons of John Jones, Talsarn throughout the morning. They are most enjoyable. We will spend the afternoon reading alternate verses. It will be very enjoyable and Tom will pontificate on some of them. We have come 130 miles since yesterday.

Monday 13 March 1882
We have a strong breeze today. It was rolling badly during the night and going full speed ahead. It is rolling less today. The wind was behind us last night and so the rolling was worse. The wind is from the side today and it is more comfortable. It is alright today and there are more birds. We are thinking of killing the pig soon. It is very fat. We have come 195 miles since yesterday.

Tuesday. 14 March 1882
It has gone much colder today. We shall have to have a fire soon. We had a bit of a calm yesterday. It will be a small day today. (*i.e. they have not travelled far.*) There are not anything like as many mice now we have the cats. We got 5 cats altogether but they all escaped ashore except for 2. One of them is

hopeless but I have never seen such a good one as the other. She is expecting kittens soon. That will not do her any harm. We have come 70 miles since yesterday.

Wednesday. 15 March 1882
I do not have much to say today. The old ship is rolling quite a bit. A very light breeze we have today. It was blowing freshly last night. I love being in rough weather and hearing the sailors singing as they handle the ropes, and the poor things have to climb the masts in the night, not seeing a hand in front of them it is so dark and blowing really hard sometimes. We have a fire today. 145 miles since yesterday and the ship is rolling. I can hardly write.

Thursday. 16 March 1882
We have had very rough seas indeed since yesterday.[24] It was blowing hard at 7 o clock last night and very dark. At 6 o'clock this morning we had to hove to as the sailors said there was too much wind for them. It is now 4 o'clock in the afternoon and the wind has died down a bit. But the sea is very high and we are starting to ship the seas. 180.

Friday. 17 March 1882
It is not blowing much today. It rolls sometimes. We are killing the pig this afternoon. The goat does not have anything like as much milk in this weather, and the hens are not laying either. I was thinking in the heavy weather the other night how comfortable it would be in Cors Iago.[25] The poor sailors are suffering, dirty and wet. We have come 68m.

Saturday. 18th March 1882
We have had a beautiful day since yesterday. The ship is rolling a lot. We will have spare ribs and potatoes for dinner today, after killing the pig yesterday. It is six weeks since we

sailed and we have made a very good passage since then; let's hope that this continues for the rest of the voyage. We have come this distance in 8 days less than the last time.[26] We have come 182 miles since yesterday.

Sunday. March 19th 1882
Here we have yet another Sunday. Thank the good Lord for that. The wind blew very hard last night, but no harder than the previous night. The little goat has hardly any milk again now in this rough weather. It looks pretty fed up. She does not like the rough weather. She shakes like a leaf. We have another week before we round the Horn as long as we keep going like this. The moon changes today. We shall have a small moon next week. 208 miles since yesterday.

Monday. March 20th 1882
We have had a strong breeze since yesterday, but not too strong, a useful wind. We sighted another ship today. I have written every day since we sailed, even though the ship has been rolling and sometimes pitching too. But she is a ship that responds very well to the sea.[27] It was snowing yesterday, showers and then heavy squalls. The same today. It is quite cold. We could be round the Horn by this time next week. 216 miles since yesterday.

Tuesday. March 21st 1882
We have a strong breeze today. We are moving ahead well these days. It will not be long now before we are round the Horn. It is pretty dull today as it is misty[28] with the odd squall. We are shortening the journey considerably in this strong, windy weather. I am not sleeping very well these nights. It is very dark and there are other ships about.[29]

N.B. There is a special misty fog around the Horn at this time of year and they could not see or hear other ships, especially at night. The thing that used to frighten Nain Langdale *more even than this, was fire at sea. Collisions around the Horn were the demise of many a ship. It was a busy shipping lane, regardless of the weather.*

Wednesday. 22 March 1882
Lighter winds today. Torrential rain and very dull. We know by the patent log[30] just how far we have come. This dull weather is difficult weather. Tom is delighted with the muffs that Sarah made him. He is thinking so much about being able to buy Cors Iago, far more than I am. It would suit him down to the ground. 175 miles since yesterday.

Dear sister,
I am very much hoping that my clothes and other things are not being ruined and that no water is getting at them to spoil them. Take care with the tea set if you move it in case it breaks. I think about you a great deal every day, and of Father, and dream about you as well, and about Tyddyn Mawr. If we can have Cors Iago I will have a lot of packing to do to come home. I have a great many things, what with the furniture and everything. I expect I shall need about three carts to meet us at the station to get them home.[31] I would rather have there than anywhere else I can think of in that area, and if we don't get it we shall be going to sea again next time. It will be very hard for Tom to leave the sea, I know they are going to raise his salary to £25.[32] I know the owners want him on the ship. They think a great deal of Tom. Captain McGill[33] told me in Newport that they do not have a captain worth calling a captain other than him. About 12 of them.[34] I only hope you are well and comfortable as are we.

Thursday. 23 March 1882
It is a clear day today. Thank God for it. We have had sun.
We are closing in on Cape Horn. I hope we can pass it quite
soon. It is cold today. I have had the homespun wool dress
on for days now. It is very warm. Tom really likes it. He likes
it best. There are plenty of birds around at the moment. We
have come 186 miles since yesterday.

Friday. 24th March 1882
It is a lovely day again today, but it is very cold. We have had
exceptionally good weather so far. But we did have one
terrible day and so we may get it again on the other side of
the Horn. I hope we don't. Today we are on the line of the
Horn and we have the sun. That is a very big thing. I get very
little milk in this cold weather. 180 miles since yesterday.

Saturday. 25th March
We have had a good day since yesterday. The great Lord is
good to us in his mercy. It is seven weeks since we sailed and
we are rounding the Horn this afternoon. It is very cold as it
always is at this time of year. We expect a good passage
home. We have come from 'Frisco to the Horn in 9 fewer
days than they came the previous time. 220 miles since
yesterday.

Sunday. 26th March 1882
We have had a fantastic day since midday yesterday. A ship
passed very close to us today. She was on a passage out with
crosswinds, poor things and fighting against the wind and
there were we with a favourable wind and the odd squall.[35] I
am much more used to heavy weather than I was on the
passage out. I am much healthier in cold weather than I am
in the hot weather. We have come 236 miles since yesterday.

Monday. 27th March 1882
Here we are alive and well, comfortable, with a favourable wind, thank God for that. It is a great boon, we really are shifting. We saw two ships today, both travelling in the same direction as us. They were too far away to see their names. It is raining today. Heavy showers. 184 miles since yesterday.

Tuesday. 28th March 1882
A beautiful day has dawned on us. We are coming along well. I think the prayers Sarah is saying on our behalf are being listened to as we are having a really good passage so far and such wonderful weather. I think Sarah is heaving like mad to bring the old ship home. I am intending to send this home to her from Queenstown as she would like to have it. 243 miles since yesterday.
N.B. Queenstown has now reverted to the old Irish name, Cobh, in S.W. Ireland.

Wednesday. 29th March 1882
We have travelled a long way since yesterday. We have a favourable wind again. A strong gale and running before the wind. There are two men at the helm.[36] We have had heavier weather before the Horn and after it than we had as we came round it. We are half way home, and we are having heavy snow showers. 230 miles since yesterday.

Thursday. 30th March
The wind is not so good today. But we have a good breeze. We have done well since yesterday. The sailors have made 2 very good mats indeed. The weather is getting a little warmer. I have finished reading John Jones, Talsarn's sermons. I wish there were more of them.[37] I have another little book that is quite good that I am reading. We have come 230 miles, the same as yesterday.

Friday. 31 March. 1882

We have had really heavy weather since yesterday, blowing and with hail and bad thunder. It is raining and the sea is really high. I can't sleep at night. But we are moving very well. We had some cross winds yesterday and last night. I just cannot write. The old ship is jumping and rolling. We have come 180 miles.

April 1st. Saturday. 1882

We have had some very wild weather for days. Blowing very hard indeed. We have not seen the sun for 2 days. We are having much worse weather here than when we were coming round the Horn. But it is also warmer here. We are all alive and well thank goodness. One of the sailors was ill yesterday, but he is much better today. 185 miles since yesterday.

Sunday. April 2nd 1882

A new Sabbath again today. It is eight weeks today since we sailed. We have had heavy weather for a week now and it is the same today. We have not seen the sun for days. The ship is rolling so much that I cannot write. I think that the sailor who was ill is better. I hope he is anyway. He is one of the best men on the ship and Tom and I are very fond of him. We have come 100.

Monday. 3 April 1882

I am glad it is better weather today. It has been pretty horrible for a week. It was blowing hard and raining and the ship was rolling and pitching and the sea was washing over her, and foggy and no sun, and the sailor who was ill fell on the deck, and the sea hit him. We think he has ruptured his diaphragm, and we can't tell whether he is better or not. I am afraid he is not. 180 miles since yesterday.

Tuesday. April 4 1882
A lovely day today with a favourable wind, thank the Lord. I think that the weather has settled by today and I am pleased to think that the sailor who was ill is getting better. He is getting every help.[38] He can have anything in the ship that he needs. Tom is a very good doctor to him. He is the one who gets up to him at night. 50 miles.

Wednesday. April 5 1882
A lovely favourable wind again today and we are moving well. We are here 10 days sooner than on the previous voyage. And we have had more bad weather than before as well. We expect to have a good passage home. I am pleased to think that the ill man is improving through some providence. I try to pray that he will get fully better, and it looks as though that will happen. 162 miles since yesterday.

Thursday. April 6th 1882
It is a fine day today. The breeze is lighter. I have been washing today. I have not done anything for a fortnight. I was washing and doing the beds. I shall do the white things another day. The sick man is coming along well, thank goodness. I am glad he is, too. 148 miles since yesterday.

Friday. 7th April 1882
The weather is much warmer. We have stopped the fire. We have not moved very much since yesterday, but we cannot complain. We have done very well so far. The sick man is getting better. I give him oranges every day. 70 miles since yesterday.

Saturday. 8 April 1882
It is 9 weeks today since we sailed from 'Frisco. The time passes quickly. It is funny to think that it is a year since I left

home. The weather is getting really hot. We are moving forward well. We have not had much cross wind on this passage. 170 miles since yesterday.

Sunday 9th April 1882

Easter Sunday. It is a beautiful day today. The wind is not too bad either. There is not much of it. We expect to pick up the trades soon.39 The weather is good, and the sun has become really hot. We did not go to our beds last night but Tom and I slept on the sofa. It is much more comfortable. We have read alternate verses today. We got up at half past five in the morning. We have come 136 miles since yesterday.

Monday. 10th April 1882

A lovely day today. It is Easter Monday. I have been washing all morning, and have put Tom's best clothes out in the sun. I have three excellent mats that the sailors have made me. The oranges are really good in this hot weather. I think I shall take some home with me if I am alive and well. I have more than I can eat. 50 miles.

Tuesday. 11th April 1882

We are in calm since yesterday. We need a really good breeze to move us on. But we must not complain as we have come as far as this particularly well. We are very comfortable even now. The ailing sailor is better and I did not think he would recover. I go to see him every day with Tom. 27 miles since yesterday.

Wednesday. 12th April 1882

We have just started to get a soft breeze. We think we have found the trades. But we have not come far since yesterday. The sun is very hot. It will get much hotter as we get closer to the line. They are filling all the holes in the ship ready for painting her so that she looks good for arriving in England.[40] I have not slept in my bed for nearly a week, only on the sofa, it's much more comfortable in this hot weather. We have done 60 miles since yesterday.

Thursday. 13th April 1882
We have a good wind today and we expect it to carry us across the line.[41] The sun is getting hotter every day. My health is fine so far, thank goodness. We have come 125 miles today. I am sending my love to you and Father.
Your sister,
    Ellen Owen

Friday. April 14th 1882
We have a good, fair wind again today. The Lord is good to us. I dream a lot about you and Father and about Tyddyn Mawr. *(i.e. my great grandmother's home. Ellen's sister, Mary, was my great grandmother)* I am afraid that there might be something the matter with you. I hope that nothing nasty is happening to you. Not many nights pass without my thinking of you. I don't expect we shall be giving up the sea if we cannot get Cors Iago. We have come 150 miles.

Saturday. April 15th 1882
A lovely wind again today. It is 12 weeks today since we sailed. We are travelling home quickly. It will not be long before we are in England. The sick man is fine now. He is working every day. I do not like this hot weather much. I sweat such a lot. You will probably be surprised to see me looking so haggard when I get home, but I can't think of going outside in this hot weather. 140 miles since yesterday.

Sunday 16th April 1882

We have not covered a great distance since yesterday. We have no cause to complain. The weather is very heavy. We have been reading this morning and we saw another ship. She was too far away to speak to her.[42] I think you are so lucky to be able to go to chapel. I am as happy as I could be at sea and I am very lucky to have seen so much of the world. Sunday is difficult. 170 miles since yesterday.

Monday 17th April 1882

We have hardly moved today. I have been washing all morning and feel much better having got something done. It is very warm. They are painting the cabins and all the rooms today. The hens are laying well at the moment. They should as they are getting plenty of food. We have 7 plus the cockerel. We shall slaughter them before getting to England. The goat is as fat as an apple. She does not have so much milk now. She had her young some time ago. She should be smaller. We have come 60 miles

Tuesday. April 18th 1882

We have had inclement weather for the last three or four days. It is very warm due to the lack of wind. The men are busy painting. I love the oranges in this hot weather. I am feeling quite tired in this hot weather as I am not sleeping very well on the sofa. The feather bed is too hot. We will be glad of it when the weather turns cold again and I can catch up on my sleep in the feathers. But there is nothing else for it for the next 3 weeks. My sides are aching after sleeping on the sofa and Tom is the same. I am very well. We have come 70 miles.

Wednesday. April 19th 1882
Slow weather today. No reason to complain. The great Lord is good to us. I dream about you every night. Why, I do not know. I am terrified of something happening to you. I hope to goodness that it does not. They are painting again today. It is time for them to finish. The smell of paint is not very nice especially in this hot weather. 60 miles since yesterday.

Thursday. April 20th 1882
Dear sister,
I am taking advantage of the present situation to write to you again today and in the hope that all is well with you as it is with us. I have nothing new to write today. I am afraid that we shall lose the time that we have gained so far. We have had a difficult time for 5 days now. If this had not happened we should have been home 2 weeks ahead of the previous time. No room for complaint. 48 miles since yesterday.

Friday. 21 April 1882
I am taking advantage of this situation to write again. We have had this wretched weather for a week now. I am afraid we shall lose the time we have made. We were 12 days ahead of ourselves until now. We are now only 9 days ahead. It is a pity to have lost ground. That is the way it is at sea especially with sailing ships. It can spoil the passage all together. A bit of a breeze. 75 miles since yesterday.

Saturday. 22 April 1882
We had a bit more wind since yesterday, but it is still very light. It is 11 weeks to yesterday since we sailed. I find that the time passes quickly from week to week. I find Sunday the worst day. It is very hot indeed today. I did lots of washing on Monday and I shall do some more today. We change our clothes so often in this weather. Sweating loads, it is as

though we had been in the river. We sleep without any clothes on now. This sweating will do me good. It moves all the ill health out of you. 97 miles since yesterday.

Sunday. 23 April
Sunday again. Thank God for it but we cannot go to chapel like you do. Tom and I have been reading alternate verses to each other. We read a lot. I have nothing to do but wash and mend. I have knitted a lot since I came to sea, and sewn a lot as well. We have a better breeze today and are nearing the line. We shall cross it next week we hope. We do not expect to be too long now before we reach England. 125 miles since yesterday.

Monday. April 24th 1882
I am very glad that we are going ahead well today. I have been washing again today and putting clean clothes on the bed, a new cover on the feather bed as well, although we will not be sleeping in it for a few weeks yet, until the weather cools although it will not get really cold. We cannot expect that. We shall go further away from the sun, it is over our heads now. This is the fourth time I have crossed the line. I have been round the world. 130 miles since yesterday.

Tuesday. April 25th 1882
We have a good wind again today but the trades on this side are not as strong as on the other side. We expect to pick up the north east trades when we have crossed the line which are stronger. If we are alive and well we shall cross the line tomorrow or the next day. It is really hot again today and it will be like this for a fortnight, and it will be fairly hot until we get home. It is nothing like as hot in England as it is here with the sun directly above our heads. I shall be glad to be in cooler weather. 148 miles since yesterday.

Wednesday. April 26th 1882
We have come a good way since yesterday. We shall cross the line early tomorrow morning. We are 9 days ahead of our previous passage. I hope we do not lose any more time on the way home. I should like to be home a few days earlier than last time. We shall come home as soon as we can. 170 miles since yesterday.

Thursday. April 27th 1882
We have crossed the line today. It is very hot. If we get a reasonable wind we could be home in 30 to 35 days. They made it in 30 days last time. But that is unusual. We will have to have a strong breeze to make it in that time to Queenstown. We shall go there for orders if the wind is favourable for that. I have 30 really good mats that the men have made and several things besides. We have come 152 miles.

Friday. April 28th 1882
We have some really heavy rain today as often occurs here. We have not really got the trades properly. There is another ship near us today and we have been talking with her, using flags, and we have beaten her by 4 days on his passage. I hope we shall get another good slant for home. The mate of the other ship has come over in his boat to get provisions that they need and that we have, and we have given them to him. 100 miles since yesterday.

Saturday. April 29th 1882
It is 12 weeks today since we sailed. We have come so well up to now, thank the Lord for that. He has been such a good Lord to us amidst such appalling dangers. The ship that was with us yesterday is with us again, and there is a wife on board until Queenstown.[43] They think that they will go

there for orders if the wind is right. We are in the doldrums[44] weather as they call it, heavy showers of rain and oppressive heat. 90 miles today.

Sunday. April 30th 1882

Yet another Sabbath. Each Sunday brings us nearer to the eternal life; the place where we shall all eventually end up. We only spend a short time in this life. I miss going to chapel on Sundays. It has rained excessively since yesterday, the worst rain since we left England. They call it the Doldrums, and the weather is sultry. We have not travelled far since yesterday. We expect to pick up the S.E. Trades. 60 miles since yesterday.

Monday. May 1st 1882

I am glad to say that we have the trades and are really moving again. I have been washing today. We have as much lovely rainwater as you could wish for to wash. I go to the bath twice a day sometimes. It is lovely. I still dream about you a lot. I was dreaming about Mary Tyddyn Mawr last night.[45] I do so hope that she and William (N.B. *my great grandparents; Tyddyn Mawr is the next farm to Cors Iago*) will be able to get Cors Iago for us. 180 miles since yesterday.

Tuesday. May 2nd 1882

We are really moving again today thanks to the good Lord. They have finished painting the cabin. We saw a ship today and we spoke with her using the flags. She was on her passage out from Swansea. We are 10 days ahead of the previous passage. I hope we do not have any accidents or it will spoil the passage, and we have come as far as this so well. It is not as warm as it was, but our butter is like oil, it is so thin. We have come 190 miles since yesterday.

Wednesday. May 3rd 1882
We have a wonderful breeze today. It is much more pleasant than it has been. It is no longer unbearably hot. I can't stand this hot, hot weather. The ship is rolling so that I can hardly write. I am busy today covering the sofa and the lockers. 202 miles since yesterday.

Thursday. May 4th 1882
A good breeze again today. We are moving home fast. There seems to be some luck with us on this passage. I hope it holds out. The ship is cutting through the water, rolling and pitching so that I cannot write. I am very busy making these sofa covers. It is strange to think that I have not been home for a year. We have come 216 miles.

Friday. May 5th 1882
The weather is much the same today. They are really busy painting and cleaning the whole of the ship. I have finished covering the sofas and they look very good. I should love it if you could see the ship, even if only once. If we came to Liverpool to unload you could come and see her. It would only take you a couple of days to get back. I expect to arrive in Queenstown in about three weeks. 226 miles since yesterday.

Saturday. May 6th 1882
Same weather again today. It is now 13 weeks since we sailed. We have come really well. I hope it pleases the good Lord that this continues. I dreamt about you a great deal again last night. I am dying to see you, and my Father, and the Tyddyn Mawr family too. We have been sleeping in the feather bed now for 2 nights. It feels wonderful after being on the sofa for so long. 221 miles.

Sunday May 7th 1882
We still have the very strong trades. We shall lose them soon. I feel pretty miserable on Sundays like this, not being able to go to chapel. We have read alternate verses again today, Tom and I. I really envy you going to chapel. I really enjoy the other days. The other days pass very quickly. We have come 205 miles.

Monday. 8th May 1882
Here we are alive and well again today. It is wonderful to have good health. There is nothing in the world like good health. I have been washing all morning. We are looking forward very much to getting Cors Iago as we have bought all this furniture, but if we don't get it we shall be going to sea again. We will be really upset if we do not get it. It will not be long before we know. 160 miles since yesterday.

Tuesday 9th May 1882
We are well today and very comfortable, a lovely breeze. We are travelling quickly towards home. I expect to be home sooner than last time by quite a few days unless something happens. We are 12 days ahead of the last voyage, and we could be home within a fortnight at this rate. I dream about you and Father. I am afraid that there is something wrong that I dream about you so much. I am thinking about you more now than I ever have since I left home. 130 miles since yesterday.

Wednesday. 10th May 1882
We have not moved very much since yesterday. It is a nuisance. I am afraid we shall be held up; and we have come so well up to now, we could still be home early. I have written every day since we left 'Frisco. If we go to sea again I shall write better notes for you. It is not always easy. 190 miles since yesterday.

Thursday. 11th May
We are in trouble today. I am afraid we shall be held up. There is nothing to be done, if that is what happens except accept the consequences. The little goat has continued to provide milk in all weathers. But it has less in bad weather. And we have been killing a hen on most Sundays for some time now. We have three left and the cockerel. We are lucky to have the cat. I have not seen such a good mouser before. The mice were everywhere before we got her. Only 29 miles since yesterday.

Friday. 12th May 1882
It looks as though we may have a bit more wind today. We have hardly moved since yesterday. The ship looks very good since she has had all this paint work done, except for the bottom.[46] My clothes are all clean and Tom's too, and mended. I wash frequently, more often than weekly. It will be good not to have so much washing to do when I get home. I never bothered about the washing until I went away, just the odd white shirt for Tom. I have been doing a bit of starching too. We have come 60 miles since yesterday.

Saturday. May 13th 1882
We are not moving very much today. We may lose the time we have made. We are coming home at a bad time of year, and having problems. But we must not complain as we may get home in the same time as on the last trip. It has been a very good passage. We have sailed 24 weeks since leaving. We could be in Queenstown in a fortnight if we get the right wind. I am afraid that you will not have written soon enough, but that is my fault. We have come 110 miles.

Sunday. May 14th 1882
We have another new Sabbath. Our time is accounted for from Sabbath to Sabbath. I am 37 years old tomorrow. I am

middle aged in my opinion. The wind is not favourable today and it is raining. We should be near Queenstown in about a fortnight. I am dying to have a letter from you, and to know how you are. We have not moved very far today. 58 miles since yesterday.

Monday. 15th May 1882
We have a cross wind today. I am afraid we shall be delayed with this. But we must not complain. The Lord has been very good to us and we do not really deserve it. I can't wait to get to Queenstown so that I can have a letter. I have been trying to pray, at least that there should not have been any bereavement. I have been dreaming about you so much. It can only be because I am thinking about you all the time. We have done 60 miles since yesterday.

Tuesday. 16th May 1882
The wind that we have today, such as it is, is a cross wind. We are hardly moving at all. We have lost the advantage that we had over the previous voyage. This is miserable. We are going further away from home instead of nearer to it. The last three days have been poor. It is a bad time of year to be coming home. 105 miles since yesterday with a cross wind for the last three days.

Wednesday. 17th May 1882
There is no end to this East wind. It is with us again today. If we had a favourable wind we should be home in 12 days, or less, even 9 or 10 days. We did not have this cross wind the last time, but we did have lots of rough weather. I ought to be a good sailor by now after going round the world. The ship is ready for England and looks in very good shape. 107 miles today.

Thursday. 18th May 1882

Cross wind again. It is awful like this. At this rate we shall be missing home altogether. There is no end to this beastly East wind. We are fed up.[47] I am pleased to tell you that my health has stood up to all this very well. So has Tom's. I am fitter than I have been since leaving home.

I am hoping for letters from you at Queenstown. 90 miles only today.

Friday. 19th May 1882

The wind is easier today. I don't feel like writing today. I have been starching and ironing all morning, and it was difficult because the ship is rolling. We have come another 110 miles.

Saturday. 20th May 1882

It is a good wind today but there is not enough of it. We are very difficult to please. The ship is rolling and pitching. There is a heavy sea. Perhaps a week to Queenstown. I really hope there is a letter for me. I cannot write today. I can't keep myself stable enough to do so. We have done 150 miles.

Sunday. 21st May 1882

It is a pretty miserable day today. It has been blowing hard since yesterday morning. The sea is high and the ship is rolling and pitching. We are nearing an island or I should say some islands.[48] It is always rough weather near these. I am almost unable to write. We are having the sort of weather that we expect round Cape Horn or the Cape of Good Hope. You are lucky being able to go to chapel today. I hope to have that pleasure very soon. 190 miles today.

Monday. 22nd May 1882
It is really blowing today. It is a good wind for us. We are
really coming home fast now. We passed 2 islands today but
we were about 20 miles away from them. High seas again
and rolling and pitching. We should be in Queenstown or
Falmouth in about a week if the wind holds. We may even be
home earlier than last time by about a week. 130 miles since
yesterday.

Tuesday. 23rd May 1882
It is good to know that we have a good, strong, favourable
wind. We are going along like a steamer. Thank the Lord for
that. Let us hope that this continues and we arrive home safely.
    I have not washed for a week because of the rolling and
pitching, but I did plenty before when we were moving
slowly. 220 miles today.

Wednesday. May 24th 1882
We have not done as well today as we did the previous day.
We must not complain about that. We are very lucky to have
done so well. I don't yet know whether I shall be coming
home from Queenstown or Falmouth. If all is well I do not
want to come before Tom. He will not like it if I go before
him unless it is to see about Cors Iago. We have come 130
miles.

Thursday. 25th May 1882
I am pleased that we are all well and that we have a suitable
wind. We are nearing home every day. We could be in
Queenstown or Falmouth within 4 or 6 days or even sooner.
We have about another 700 miles to go. We have done very
well so far. We do not yet know where we shall be going to
unload, not until we get our orders.[49] The ship is tidy and
spotless. She looks really good. 160 miles since yesterday.

Friday. May 26th 1882
It is blowing really hard again today and we are moving fast. I can hardly write again due to the rolling and pitching. 200 miles today.

Saturday. 27th May 1882
The wind is favourable today. We are nearing Queenstown quickly and I can hardly sleep with the rolling and pitching. We shall be in Queenstown tomorrow night in the middle of the night. Not many make this passage from 'Frisco in 3 and a half months. You may not be expecting us. We are 8 or 9 days ahead of the previous voyage. We have come 221 miles since yesterday.

Sunday. 28th May 1882
It is a beautiful day today and very clear. We cannot get to Queenstown tonight as the wind is lighter. It is still in our favour. I do not expect there will be a letter from you as I did not expect to be home as soon as this. I shall send this to you. I shall send a note to Father too. The ship is rolling again. She is a good ship in a rough sea. 148 miles today.

Monday. 29th May 1882
I am pleased to tell you that we are all well. We are very near Queenstown. We are not moving quickly as the wind is light but it is favourable. The pilot has been with us since 7 o'clock this morning. We are only moving 3 or 4 miles an hour. We shall be in some time tonight. It might have been last night if the wind had been stronger. We are moving along the Irish coast. It is a beautiful day. We have come 80 miles.

Monday. 30th May. 1882
Dear Sister,

I am pleased to tell you that we are all well and that we have arrived safely.

I do not have time to write more. Tom is going ashore and wishes to be remembered to you.

Your loving sister,

Ellen Owen

I shall write again when we get our orders.

Saturday. 4th June. 1882.[50]

Chapter 5

Minafon

The orders Ellen mentioned in her diary arrived. The *Cambrian Monarch* sailed for Limerick, and started unloading on 13th June 1883.[1] By the 18th July she was in London[2] and at about this time Captain Owen had the opportunity to go home to Tudweiliog. The *Cambrian Prince*, under the command of Captain D. Davies, sailed for Sydney from London on June 16th just one week after the *Cambrian Princess*, with Captain Bailey, also sailed for Sydney. In the same edition of Lloyd's Weekly Shipping Index, 23rd June 1882, there is account of the *Monarch* reaching Limerick, the *Prince* and *Princess* passing Prawle Point and the *Queen* arriving in the Thames. The *Monarch* sailed again for Melbourne on September 1st, but there is no definite information about the captain. By 1884 Captain Thomas Owen had moved to the *Cambrian Princess* and Captain T. Williams to the *Monarch*. Sometime between July 1882 and the time he sailed on the *Princess* Thomas Owen had time to build a new home for Ellen.

Cors Iago was a homestead of 5 acres standing between the Tudweiliog Mill and Tyddyn Mawr and less than half a mile from Ellen's home, Tyddyn Sander. The right hand turning from the main Tudweiliog to Aberdaron road that leads down to Porth Ysgadan goes past Cors Iago. It is about 100 yards from the old Cors Iago house that Thomas Owen built his new home.

In his classic book, *Hen Longau Sir Gaernarfon*[3] David Thomas talks about the 'new captains' that came from the sailing ships to be senior managers of the Liverpool steam ship companies, Cunard, Elder Dempster and Blue Funnel. In between the sailing ship era and the era of the steamer there were some captains who were in the service of the Liverpool Welsh community and who became spokesmen for that group which David Thomas describes so well. 'These new captains were dignified men, well dressed, in uniform, with brass buttons and with elegant new villas. They were good businessmen who understood the world and how it worked, with authority and confidence in their bearing. Ready, also, for a chat over their cigars, reminiscing over their grandfathers who were masters of sailing ships and about their youth when they were apprenticed on those ships'. Captain Thomas Owen, the son of the Tudweiliog miller, was one such man.

As you look at Minafon today it is easy to see why Thomas Owen was so pleased with his new home. A large, square, solid house with four bedrooms, one of which was a library. It had a garden, and a wall, with a small river running between the house and the garden, over a small bridge to his workshop in the old Cors Iago dwelling. Maybe the most significant thing is the engraving of the anchor in the side of the great chimney with the date 1883 above it. It is as clear today as it was when the house was built more than 100 years ago. Thomas Owen designed the house himself and it was said in Tudweiliog that he had brought Liverpool style to Tudweiliog with high, stylish ceilings. He was a comparatively young man at the time, being 37 years old and still going to sea. It was clear that Thomas Owen's ability would take him further. Minafon was just one more step on the road. Despite that it was an important step. It meant that he and his wife had their own home base to which they could come at any time. It was to Minafon that the San Francisco furniture would come from the hold of the *Cambrian Monarch*. It was here that Richard Davies, Weirglodd Fawr, the carpenter from the *Cambrian Monarch*, made the shelves for the Captain's library, and the beautiful

Richard Davies, Weirglodd Fawr, the carpenter on the Cambrian Monarch *and his wife, Ann. Ann was Captain Thomas Owen's sister*

rosewood cupboard, a wonderful example of the skill of the ship's carpenters of that time. As it happened the cupboard was too big to go upstairs and so it remained in the kitchen although it was a beautiful piece of furniture. Over the years Thomas Owen spent many hours in the workshop in Cors Iago, and the maid used to light a fire for him there. He used to listen for the sound of the Tyddyn Mawr children coming over the bridge; the children of Ellen's sister, Mary, who would come to hear stories and be given the odd present.

(N.B. This includes Elizabeth Janet who later married Owen Williams, Hirdre Fawr, and became my paternal grandparents.) Before Thomas Owen was able to settle down in Minafon there was a great deal more travelling to be done.

By 1883/4 Lloyd's Register shows that Captain Bailey had left the *Cambrian Princess* and that Captain Owen had taken his place, being replaced on the *Monarch* by Captain T. Williams. The years on the *Princess* were very successful. On the 1884 voyage attention was drawn to Captain Owen in nautical circles because he observed a sand shoal which had not appeared in the charts. The *Princess* was en route from Queensland to Adelaide when the bank was spotted three miles long and eight feet high at position 15°44'S 149°41'E. The Hydrographic Department of the Admiralty was informed and a warning to mariners circulated (Notice to Mariners. No. 9, 1884.), naming the bank as Owen Bank Islet. Another voyage showed that Captain Owen had sailed through a channel in the Great Barrier Reef which had not been measured and he declared it to be far clearer of coral than the usual channel, the Trinity channel. These are the seas that the Frenchman, Louis Antoine de Bouganville, sailed in 1768 when he circumnavigated the world in 1766/1769. After Captain Owen's announcement a survey was conducted by the ship *Myrmydion* under Commander R. Hoskyn. They decided that the Diane Bank described by de Bouganville in 1768 and the Owen sandbank were very close together and should be regarded as one. The Owen description was more accurate than de Bouganville's because the latter admitted that he had seen the bank at twilight and from some distance. The Hydrographic Department therefore decided to keep the original name Diane Bank rather than Owen Bank Islet. In September 1892 Thomas Owen had a letter from Captain Wharton, R. N. F.R.S., the hydrographer, apologising that they had not let him know that they had decided to keep the original name but '*as to you, mariners are indebted for the true position of this bank*'.[4]

It is obvious from Ellen Owen's diary that Thomas Owen is determined to better himself in Thomas Williams' company and Captain McGill supports him. In a later entry when Captain Owen went out to San Francisco in the nineties to take one of the ships over for a short time it was his last voyage as an employee of the Thomas Williams' company. He had moved from the *Princess* in 1888. He had a shore job, possibly taking over from Captain McGill, for the next 4 years, overseeing the ships in port. By the beginning of the nineties it seems that it was time to re-organise the company that was operating from Oriel Chambers, 14, Water St. Liverpool. Captain Thomas

Williams' son was not really interested in the company and they wanted to re-register their ships as 'single ship companies'. Thus on February 12th 1891 it was announced that the Thomas Williams' company had taken on 2 new partners, Mr Samuel Roberts and Captain Thomas Owen.

> 'Mr Roberts has been in the employ of the firm for the last 20 years and is therefore fully conversant with the business of the firm.
>
> Captain Owen has also been connected with us for 18½ years and has for some time past filled a position of trust in the office.
>
> Their varied and practical experience will still further insure the protection of the interests of all with whom we have relation.
>
> The business will be carried on under the same name as before and we hope to receive a continuance of the support.'[5]

This, therefore, is the company that Professor J. Glyn Davies went to work for as a clerk; and this is the source of the sea shanties on which Welsh children were brought up. *(N.B. Including me. The book* Cerddi Huw Puw *is in Nain's piano stool!)* In the essay written as an introduction to the book, 'Shanties and Sea Songs on Welsh Ships', certainly one of the best pieces ever written about Welsh ships, we have a first rate description of life in the shipping world of Liverpool, his days as an apprentice in the Rathbone Bros. offices, and then of the time he spent in the Thomas Williams Co. (and thus as a clerk with the new partner Thomas Owen.), as shown by the following excerpt.

> 'In 1892, when I entered the office of my old friend, T. G. Williams, I was plunged in the midst of Welsh ships and Welsh seamen; and there were real old timers

amongst them, who served on the old Black Ball Line. The founder of the firm, Captain Thomas Williams, had been overlooked for the Black Ball line, and when the owners came to grief he bought up a number of the ships and manned them with Welshmen.

The pomp and circumstance of the Black Ball Line was spoken of with bated breath as something that had been and would never be again; great clipper ships, manned like racing yachts, with vivid tales of races home with new season's teas, and of marvellous passages to Melbourne. The hulls were things of beauty, such as would never be seen again; the lines from stem to stern could only be described by one tense word – beautiful! Even the more prosaic iron ships, with a minimum number of crew allowed by law, carried a tangible reminder of piracy in the China seas, in the musket racket'.

The year that J. Glyn Davies[6] started working in the company offices, a new ship was ordered, the first for some years, so reinforcing the confidence in the large, steel ships being built in the nineties. Among the most famous ships in this class that were built for Welsh companies were the *Republic, Dominion, Natia,* and the *Annie Thomas* for the William Thomas, Liverpool, company; the *Celtic Queen,* the *Celtic Race* and the *Carnedd Llewellyn* for R. Hughes-Jones, Liverpool; the *Conway Castle, Penrhyn Castle* and the *Powis Castle* for R. Thomas, Cricieth and Liverpool. All large, steel ships or barques. *(N.B. In this context the term ship or barque refers to the rig of the craft. Langdale was a 'full rigged ship' having square rig on all masts; the Grenada was a four masted barque, being square rigged on three masts and fore and aft rigged on the mizzen (rear) mast.)* The *Cambrian Hills,* a steel, full rigged ship, was ordered from the Rodger's yard in Glasgow and a single ship company was formed in order to pay for her with 167 shares of £100 each.

The original group who formed the company included Thomas Griffith Williams, 14, Water St. Liverpool; Samuel Roberts, Hazeldean, Hoylake; Thomas Owen, Minafon, Tudweiliog; Thomas Scott, 14, Woodside, Sunderland, all described as 'Shipowner'; Eleazer Roberts, Preswylfa, Hoylake, magistrates clerk; Henry Thomas, 22, Bank Quay, Caernarfon, Master mariner, and Richard Jones, Anfield, Purser.7 The Thomas Williams Company was to manage the ship from their offices in Oriel Chambers, and were to take 2.5% of the profits. Captain Henry Thomas from Caernarfon was the man who had been a master mariner sailing for the William Thomas company, and had been the marine superintendent in the Falklands.

'The arrival of the *Cambrian Queen* in the Mersey in 1893 gave me my first live interest in shanties. She was anchored in the Sloyne and I went off on the tug with Captain Henry Thomas who was to take her into the Albert Dock at 2a.m. It was a brilliant moonlit night, and I stood with the captain on the poop, watching the men weighing anchor. They sang 'Aroving' and whether from this vivid association or whether from the intrinsic worth of the melody, I do not know or care but to me it is the finest of all the shanties. Captain Thomas was an excellent singer, with a great stock of songs, and during the time the ship was in dock I picked up some shanties from him. My brother, Captain Frank Davies, now of Shanghai, joined the *Queen* on her outward voyage and on his return I got practically the rest of my present repetory of sea songs and shanties. Three years ago my brother and I sang over all the shanties we knew; there was not a note of difference between us, and the few shanties in this book may be taken as pretty accurate records.'8

There were many single ship companies at this time, the same people being partners in each one, but in 1895 it became clear that Samuel Roberts and Thomas Owen were ready to run their own company, and therefore to buy their own ships. The first ship that the Roberts Owen company of 28, Chapel St. Liverpool, bought was the *Carnarvon Bay*, built at the Rodgers yard in Port Glasgow in 1894, and one of the new, steel, fully rigged sailing ships. Samuel Roberts was responsible for the office and Captain Owen for the ships. He travelled a great deal to make sure that they made a profit for the shareholders from North Wales and from the Welsh community in Liverpool. When the Cambrian ships were sold in 1895 Roberts Owen bought the *Cambrian King*. In less than 5 years they were managing the *Moel Eilian*, *Moel Tryvan* and the *Moel y Don* previously owned by the Gwynedd Shipping Company.

According to the article on the *Moel Tryvan* in *Maritime Wales* 1984, the only blot on the landscape at this time was the official enquiry into the loss of the *Moel Tryvan*, her captain and some of her crew in 1901. It was said that it was not possible to bring charges against Samuel Roberts as he was not in Antwerp when the ship sailed and he was not a qualified mariner. But Captain Thomas Owen was a master mariner of 20 years experience and he was responsible for loading the *Moel Tryvan* with the silver sand that was her ballast cargo for the fatal trip. There was a great deal of discussion about the case and questions asked in the senate, and manuals of the official enquiry were produced when Captain Owen won his case. He claimed that he took every reasonable precaution that any shipowner would to load the ship and he won his claim against the insurers. This episode may have detracted from Minafon at the time but there is no doubt that Captain Owen became a highly regarded master mariner/shipowner in Liverpool and North Wales. In 1902

The Langdale. *Captain Griffith Jones, Pwllheli, one of the ships owned by Captain Thomas Owen and Samuel Roberts, Liverpool*

another steel barque was purchased to replace the *Moel Tryvan* and when the *Cambrian King* was lost she was replaced by the barque *Centurion*, built by Russells of Greenock in 1891. In 1904 the *Langdale* was bought by Roberts Owen and company through Kellocks for £8,250.[9] She was bought as one of their single ship company vessels, the Moel Tryvan Ship Co. 'having its main place of business at 19, Old Hall St. Liverpool'. Samuel Roberts and Thomas Owen moved from Chapel St. to Old Hall St. in 1896 and they were there for the next 20 years. In 1908 they also bought the *Forest Hill* a large iron ship built by W. H. Potter of Liverpool, the same company that built the *Langdale* and their old friend, Captain W. Hansord was made master of the *Forest Hill*.

In the shipping world of that time it was necessary to have backers, and Roberts Owen and Co. were in competition with other shipping companies having Welsh interests. Looking at the list of shareholders loyal to this company it is seen that many come from the Llŷn and Pwllheli area and others are those associated with the Liverpool shipping scene such as chandlers, sailmakers and rope manufacturers. When the *Moel Tryvan* was bought as a single ship company in 1900[10] it was necessary to pay the £8,500 bill, and 885 shares of £10 each were thus for sale. By

August 1900, 718 were taken up. Those registered were as follows; Eleazer Roberts, Hoylake; George Edwards, Accountant, Lord St. Liverpool; Burnall and Co. Sailmakers, Liverpool; Grayson and Co. Shipbuilders, Liverpool; MacSymons Stores Ltd; John Holman and Co. shipowners. There were also shipowners from Wales such as Captain Huw Roberts from Edern who was a shipowner in Newcastle-on-Tyne, and Robert Thomas from Nefyn and Cricieth by now a Liverpool shipowner. There were also some independent shareholders such as George Davies, warehouse manager from Bolton; H. R. Williams, butcher, Penmaenmawr; Owen John Owen, Methodist minister, Rockferry; Alfred Tucker, Wesleyan minister; Owen Brown, Everton, surgeon; Robert Davies, Terfyn, Nefyn, farmer; William Griffith, Penlan Bach, Pwllheli, shipmaster, *(N.B. Nain* Langdale's *brother, Uncle Will, Captain of the* Carnarvon Bay*)* Charles Henry Bailey, Newport, master mariner; Mary Jones Griffith, Penlan Bach, Pwllheli, schoolmistress. *(Nain's sister.)* and Ellen Owen, Minafon, Tudweiliog, married woman.

Thomas Owen was a close friend of the Penlan Bach family so it was quite natural for Ellen to have some shares in her own name. Captain Evan Jones, Caernarfon, who was lost at sea shortly after this was the biggest shareholder with 60 shares. There were often relatives amongst shareholders such as Sarah Williams, Tyddyn Sander, Ellen's sister, and these were later inherited by Mary, her other sister.

One of the things that strikes one as one reads about this maritime history of Wales are the close ties between the shipowners and their captains; and between the captains and their crews, who were often chosen from the captain's home port. When a captain became a shipowner the practice would then continue; Captain Thomas Owen chose captains from Pwllheli i.e. Captain William Griffith, the *Carnarvon Bay* and Captain Griffith Jones the *Langdale*, both connected to the Penlan Bach family and both outstanding masters. The Penlan Bach and Minafon families were great friends and not only because Captain Owen left his pony and trap in Penlan Bach whenever he came to Pwllheli from Tudweiliog, but because Captain Owen knew about mariners.

About 20 years ago a Holyhead man, Commodore Gerald N. Jones, O.B.E., D.S.O. wrote about the ships that used to come into Holyhead under sail when he was a boy and about one morning in particular when the schoolboys went down to watch the *Carnarvon Bay* come in. 'The four masted barque, *Carnarvon Bay* sailed into the harbour, the master, a man from Pwllheli handling her in a superb manner and throwing her up into the wind as though she were a small boat. It was blowing a gale at the time too.'[11] Ellen Owen knew the Penlan Bach family well and was able to compare notes about rounding the Horn with Mrs Jones *Langdale* although the daughter of Penlan Bach had been there far more often than Ellen Owen herself. I have mentioned earlier about Ellen Jones Griffith who married Captain Griffith Jones, *Langdale*, and sailed with her husband and children at least 6 times round the Horn in the *Langdale*. On her first voyage she saw the Horn five times in 6 weeks as the *Langdale* battled her way round against the storms.

As one looks at the lovely painting done in 1905 of the *Langdale* by Mohrmann[12] and reads the log in the Henry the Eighth's arsenal at Woolwich, which houses part of the archives belonging to the maritime museum at Greenwich, one gets the feeling of a very different voyage from that described earlier by Ellen Owen. The *Langdale* sailed from Liverpool on the 30th January 1904, a few hours after Captain Griffith Jones married Ellen Jones Griffith, the daughter of Penlan Bach, Pwllheli. *(N.B. Penlan Bach is where the Chartered Surveyors Yale and Hemmings had their offices in Penlan St. The arch of the entrance is clear. It was a pub and my great grandmother was the licensee with my great grandfather running a road haulage business from there.)* Ellen remained behind as her husband sailed via Glasgow to Hongay in China. Other than the captain on that voyage the crew consisted of:

John Rowland Williams, second mate, from Pwllheli
Hugh Ellis Evans, ship's carpenter, from Borth-y-Gest
George F. Thomas, steward, from Porthmadog
Ben Jones, cook, from Porthmadog
R. G. Evans, sailmaker, from Porthmadog
Thomas E. Roberts, from Porthmadog joined the ship in Glasgow as second mate, coming from the *Carnarvon Bay*
Owen Roberts from Amlwch, third mate
A young, 17 year old sailor, from Nefyn

Captain Griffith Jones was a proven and hardened sailor, 37 years old, born in Nefyn on January 23rd 1867, 5'8" tall, fairly dark *(N.B. My mother said he had red hair as a young man as did my other grandfather, Hirdre Fawr. My parents thought I would have red hair too!)* He went to sea as a 'boy', aged 13 on the *Elizabeth Beck*, a Nefyn schooner and then on the smack *Fishguard Lass*, a small ship carrying manganese from the Llŷn peninsula. Captain Jones sailed on several other coasters until he 'went deep sea' on the *Cambrian Queen*, the *Pengwern*, the *Lady Penrhyn* and the *Queen of Cambria*. In 1885 he was caught by crimps in San Francisco but escaped from them to pass the exams and become second mate in 1892. He was first mate on the *Bass Rock* and the *Gantock Rock* before passing Captain and joining the *Langdale* in 1904.[13]

Some of the crew, none of whom were Welsh, left the

ship in Glasgow, and when the ship sailed she carried half Welsh and half Scandinavian crew. On the 21st June 1904 the *Langdale* arrived in Hongay. There the sailmaker and one of the A.B.s jumped ship. The *Langdale* proceeded to sail in ballast to Portland, Oregon and arrived in November 1904. In Portland the 3rd mate went on a spree and returned to the ship ready to have a go at the captain. 'He insulted me, the Master, by calling me lots of names and touching me on the chest with his hand and on being told that he was threatening a sick man he replied he would finish me by knocking the wind out of me, therefore I fined him 10 shillings for going on shore and 5 shillings for the assault.' *(This does not quite make sense but I think Taid would have no truck with a difficult crewman. I presume the 'sick man' was another crew member, or it could have been Taid.)* Things went from bad to worse and a week later Owen Roberts was discovered in a drunken state and threatening to kill the captain. He was discharged the ship forthwith. About a week after they sailed from Oregon one of the crew, William Goulding, dropped a bucket on to the back of another man, and would not admit he had done it, nor apologise. Goulding was a Barbados man and the episode seemed to affect his reason; he felt that the entire crew and the officers were against him. Although the captain tried to persuade him otherwise there was no changing him and he went to the second mate and told him that this was to be his last day on earth. The captain investigated the matter immediately and was told that Goulding felt someone was going to murder him. 'He told me that someone forrard was going to hurt him and that they were all down on him because he was a black man and over that affair with the bucket.' The captain gave him room in his own cabin overnight and gave him some whisky with 10 drops of laudanum in it to make him sleep, and locked him in the cabin. It was New Years Eve and the crew met on the poop at midnight to celebrate. The captain asked them about Goulding and they said it was all in his imagination because he was the only black man on board. The captain then told them that G. was downhearted and to try and cheer him up a bit. G. appeared from the cabin at 7a.m. and seemed fine after a good night's sleep, working happily with the rest of the crew, but an hour later at the change of watch Captain Griffith Jones heard a voice call 'Goodbye all hands'. They changed course immediately and the captain threw him a lifebelt but G. made no effort to save himself. The captain later heard that G. had told some of the crew that he was afraid of returning home, but it was too late to do anything more. Two weeks after this the carpenter, from Porthmadog, refused to turn out and help the crew with tacking the ship, and the following day one of the Scandinavians refused to turn out. The *Langdale* reached Antwerp in May 1905[14] and Mrs Jones was there to meet her husband. *(I should think he was glad to see her! This must have been when he bought her the painting.)* He stayed at sea under sail for the next 10 years.

Ellen Jones recalls her first voyage home from San Francisco as being very different from that of Ellen Owen on the *Cambrian Monarch*. They left 'Frisco for Eureka, just missing the 1906 earthquake, but feeling the tremors at sea. From Eureka they sailed to Guayaquil, Ecuador and on to Iquique and thence home round the Horn. Several icebergs were seen in the vicinity of the Falklands. *(Nain told me that she saw 14 in all and that Taid had called her on deck to see them.)* Ellen Jones was not on the *Langdale* for the next voyage, which was just as well because the ship suffered terribly in a bad storm rounding the Horn, losing masts and spars.[15] *(We have a card at home showing the damage. The picture is also in the ship's wheel frame, which the carpenter made for Nain.)* She had to put into Montevideo for repairs. This did not put Mrs Jones off at all, and she travelled by the steamer *Ortega* to rejoin her husband in Montevideo. On the round trip home Moraned was born. Whilst they were in Sydney, Australia the officers on the ship gave Moraned a doll. It was named Sydney. *(It later became my doll, but she was not very pretty by then as Aunty Helen had used her as well and she had cut her hair, thinking it would grow. I was proud of Sydney because she had brown eyes like me and no-one else had a doll with brown eyes. This was 1940 and there were very few dolls around due to it being wartime.)* The sailmaker made clothes for Moraned. She was very proud of them but she could not sit down in them because he made them of sail canvas and it was very stiff indeed. I can imagine Ellen Jones having a good laugh in later years as she looked at her discharge certificates. I have 2 on the desk in front of me as I write this page, stating that Ellen G. Jones, aged 36, born in Pwllheli, would leave *Langdale* on April 1st 1910 at Queenstown following her voyage as 'stewardess' which began in Hamburg on May 21st 1909, and that she was of good character (V.G.). This was given to most of the crew unless they had been a real problem and 'got their name in the log'. Ellen Jones said her husband said that in her case it stood for 'very talkative'! The other certificate I have shows that she travelled on the *Grenada* as a 'stewardess' also from Newcastle on July 11th to the south-west coast of South America and the voyage ended for her in Plymouth on 25th March 1914. The first world war was imminent and Moraned and her mother had left the ship some time before she was taken in the Channel by a German battleship in 1916. Captain Griffith Jones and his crew landed in Eastbourne in small boats, so ending his career in sail. *(He became Lieut. Griffith Jones R.N.R. i.e. Royal Naval Reserve during the war. After that he served in steamers and finally took a steamer, S. S. Itanage, out to Rio from Glasgow for a S. American company. He and his wife and daughter lived in Rio until his retirement in 1930. He must, therefore, have had a master mariner's certificate in sail and in steam, but I have never seen the latter.)*

Before going further we must look at the company of Thomas Owen and Samuel Roberts again. The *Carnarvon Bay* was lost in bad weather near King's Island, Bass Strait, on a journey to Australia in 1910. The entire crew was saved after spending several hours in open boats. *(This is documented in* Maritime Wales *No. 8.)* If we look at the list of shareholders for the ship *Carnarvon Bay* in January 1912, i.e. the company that bought the barque *Torrisdale* to replace the *Bay*, we see that they are the same as the 1906 register:

> Thomas Owen, Minafon, the main shareholder, with 218 shares.
> Samuel Roberts, Hoylake, increased his holding from 96 to 324 shares.
> William Griffith, Penlan Bach, Pwllheli, Captain, 60 shares. *(Uncle Will)*
> Ellen Griffith Jones, Langdale, 25 shares. *(Nain Langdale)*
> Mary Edwards Jones, Captain Griffith's sister, 25 shares. *(Aunty Mary, Penlan)*
> Elizabeth Griffith, Captain Griffith's oldest sister, 25 shares.[16] *(Aunty Bet)*

Many other people held shares in the company, but companies such as the Marine Trust Ltd, Liverpool also held shares. The price of sailing ships was very low before the first world war broke out and Roberts Owen maintained their fleet by buying ships comparatively cheaply. The *Bay* cost £15,500 in 1894. The *Torrisdale*[17] took her place in 1910 and cost £5,216. She was lost with all hands on December 23rd 1912. *(Uncle Will was first officer. Thus Nain Langdale lost her brother)* A new company was formed, the Gwalia Shipping Co. to buy the large steel sailing ship *Grenada*.

Between 1906 and 1913 there was a great change in the

price of sailing ships, dropping from £4/£5 a ton to £1.12/£2.10 a ton in 1909 and rising to £3.00 a ton in 1910. Over 150 sailing ships were sold to Scandinavian owners between 1910 and 1911, and as the war loomed the demand for ships increased again. In the book *Ships and Seamen of Anglesey* I read about the famous sailing ship *Oweenee*. She belonged to the Lewis and Heron Co. and was captained by Captain Robert Jones of Amlwch.[18] He left the ship in Hamburg in April 1910, and she was sold in 1911[19] for £3,700. By 1913, when she was bought by Roberts Owen they had to pay £9,374, but they would think that a fair price for such a wonderful ship. The *Oweenee* was the largest ship for them to own and manage, a 4 masted, steel barque 309/42/24.6. Captain Owen did not deal in small ships. The master of the *Oweenee* in 1913 was J. Collins, the mate at the time Captain Robert Jones, Amlwch. There is a good photo of Captain Collins in the collection of his friend, Captain Griffith Jones, *Langdale*, and also of the *Oweenee* and the *Grenada* taking on coal in Newcastle, N. S. Wales, in 1912. *(The year the* Titanic *went down.)*

The number of shares owned by Thomas Owen in the 'Bay' company had not changed at all over the years, but Samuel Roberts had over 500 shares by 1917, most of which had been bought cheaply before the war from the original shareholders of the *Carnarvon Bay*. The prices of these ships had risen by £10 a ton during the war. The *Oweenee* was sold in 1917 to the Hudson Bay Company, and the *Langdale* in 1916.[20] When the *Carnarvon Bay* Co. was wound up in 1917 it was discovered that Samuel Roberts was the sole partner, showing that Thomas Owen had given up managing ships about 1915, for the simple reason that there was nothing else to do as the *Langdale* had been sold, the *Grenada* sunk and the *Oweenee* idle after reaching Birkenhead in 1915.

However, Thomas Owen himself was not idle in his home patch, and the school and the chapel in Tudweiliog benefited from his philanthropy between the years of 1907 and when he died in 1919. In the managers book for Tudweiliog school it shows that Captain Owen was present at their first meeting on June 22nd 1908 and that he had been elected as a visiting manager 'as per rule 9 in the handbook'. In January 1911 he became the treasurer and in March 1911 'correspondent'.[21] Up to now the reports had all been brief, but from then on the hand of the old captain was clear. Everything was noted in detail in his own hand. English was, of course, the language used at this time and Captain Owen using phrases such as 'forthwith' or 'extending the right hand of friendship' showed his maritime business background time and time again.

He was zealous in this task as in all others and rarely missed a meeting, although the odd entry in the minutes shows that he was still involved in the shipping business.

Captain and Mrs Thomas Owen in later days in Minafon, when he was so philanthropic to the chapel and the school in Tudweiliog

The way ahead for the school, the sewerage system, contagious diseases, prizes and medals for the children, the odd discussion with the attendance officer in Caernarfon, were all given the same attention as was given to the business of managing ships, but the thing that gave him the most pleasure was talking to the children about his travels. I wonder what the reaction of the children was to this tall man who had sailed the world. He would certainly have prepared his lessons well.

In an article in *Y Traethodydd*[22] twenty years previously entitled 'The Wide Open Sea', Captain Owen showed his interest in statistics, geography, history, literature, and the Bible; today's reader should remember that he was self taught, having gone to sea before the mast as a boy, reading and learning in his spare time. The diary shows that Ellen was happy to accept her husband's view of things. She also took an interest in the school in Tudweiliog, attending the prizegivings and other functions. Reading between the lines it seems that Tom treated the school with the same importance as the ships, and Ellen supported in the background as ever.

Captain Owen was a man who took his responsibilities seriously. 'March 17th 1914, Captain T. Owen (school manager) called at 11.10 a.m. and stayed some time and watched the teachers and scholars at work'. The school walls also reflected his interest. It is said that pictures of the *Cambrian Monarch* and the *Cambrian Princess* adorned the walls at one time, but they have since disappeared. Another example of an entry in the school log-book reads 'Sept. 14th 1910, Captain Owen, Minafon presented a picture of the *Carnarvon Bay* to the school'. Again this picture has gone missing. One of his gifts, however, is in the school even today; 'Sept. 8th 1914. A beautiful piano presented to the school by Captain Thomas Owen F.R.G.S., Minafon arrived here this evening from Liverpool'. He was there the next morning to check that all was well. The piano is there to this day with the inscription 'Presented by Captain Thomas Owen, F.R.G.S., Minavon, to Tudweiliog council school, 1918'. The maker was K. Bord, Paris. Generations of children will have sung to that piano by now *(including my father who used to walk to school from Hirdre Fawr; Aunty Bet, Cefn Isa, told me that he never walked with the rest of them but always on his own and that he was different from the rest of the family. He always seemed to me to be more like Aunty Minafon's family and she was certainly his favourite aunt, his mother's sister.)*

The storm clouds of the first world war then began to cast their shadow over even such an unlikely place as Tudweiliog, and Captain Owen was now starting to write letters to the boys who had been in his Sunday School class and who were away in distant countries fighting a battle that was none of their making; and in the trenches.[23]

It seems that the lifestyle of his latter years took precedence over the years of being a shipmaster and later a shipowner. After his death the obituary in the *Herald Gymreig* referred to Captain Thomas Owen F.R.G.S., but the only mention made regarding the sea was that the hymn, 'Ar fôr tymhestlog teithio'r wyf' was sung in Minafon at the funeral. *(This was also sung at Nain and Taid Langdale's funerals and my Mother's in Liverpool.)* No mention was made of the fact that he was a master in a million. No mention either of his voyage on the *British India* at the time of the war in the Pacific. Nor indeed of the discovery of the Owen Bank when master of the *Cambrian Princess*. Nor, again, that he owned and managed such great ships as the *Langdale*, the *Grenada*, the *Moel Tryvan* and the *Oweenee*, the *Carnarvon Bay*, and the rest. The account in the *Herald* only talks about his love of the 'Gymanfa Ganu' and his favourite hymns.[24]

Ellen was a tremendous support to Tom throughout the years, in Liverpool and in Tudweiliog, in the shipping world and at home in Minafon, in the school and the chapel. She did not seek publicity herself, but she is very much remembered in the family; a lady in the true sense of the word, much loved by the local children; busy looking after Minafon helped by Bagillt, the servant, when Tom was away. Tom was ill for some months before he died on Whit Sunday, June 8th 1919, aged 72. Ellen stayed in Minafon for many years afterwards. She died, aged 85, on February 20th 1931 and was buried with her husband in the churchyard in Tudweiliog. *(Their gravestone is easy to find as it is made of granite, is high, and is on the right side of the church path as you pass the church from the main gate.)*

Mrs Ellen Owen with her niece, Mrs Ellen Sara Parry Jones (Mary, Tyddyn Mawr's daughter). Taken on holiday in Carmarthen in 1921

The clouds of another war were gathering, and the days of sailing with Tom to Australia, San Francisco and round the Horn belonged to another age. The sailing ships were all being sold and the *Cambrian Monarch* was the last of the *Cambrians* to go. I wonder if Ellen used to walk down to Porth Ysgaden in her old age and think of those lovely sailing ships that she had known in her lifetime; the *Cambrian Monarch*, the *Cambrian Princess*, the *Langdale* and the *Oweenee*.

It is very rarely that events outside the school are recorded in the school register and log, but the headmaster wrote in the log of Tudweiliog school on a sunny day in June 1919. 'June 11th 1919. Griffith Roberts, 4½ years, admitted this morning. The burial of one of our managers and correspondent for many years, Captain Thomas Owen, F.R.G.S., Minafon, takes place at 2.0p.m. today'.

There is an end to every voyage.

Appendix A

Captain Thomas Owen wrote the article 'The Wide Open Sea' for *Y Traethodydd* XLIX 1893 pages 23-28. This was about the time he was expanding his interests as a ship owner and had been accepted as a partner in Thomas Williams' Company at Liverpool. The article shows that Captain Owen was one of the mariners who had spent a lot of their time at sea – reading and educating themselves. I believe the article reveals much about the author and his society.

THE WIDE OPEN SEA

Looking back at the history of the world, we discover that man's knowledge relating to the shape and size of the earth developed very gradually. The general belief for thousands of years was that the earth was flat and that there was an end to this flatness over which it was possible to fall.

We realise that it was not the purpose of the Bible to teach Geography; because of that, we must consider many of the pictures relating to the Creation – such as the 'pillars' of heaven and earth mentioned in Job (IX 6 and XXVI 11), – as figurative or poetic and also expressions of the beliefs which were common at the time they were written. But despite that, we can see in the same book (XXVI 7) a truth about the creation not discovered for a long time after the author's death. It is said of God – 'He stretches the north over the void and hangs the earth upon nothing.' It was impossible at the time for any man to even imagine the fact which by now is known, that indeed, the earth does 'suspend on nothing.'

If we compare the distribution of the earth which appears in the 10th chapter of Genesis with the 'extremities' of the earth mentioned at the meeting of the Queen of Sheba with Solomon, we can see that understanding of Geography increased slowly. It was believed that the Queen of Sheba's home at the earth's extremity from which she came to hear of Solomon's wisdom, was in the southernmost part of the Arabian Peninsula between the Red Sea and the Indian Ocean.

Again if we look at a world map of the 10th century B.C. when Homer wrote his epics, we can see that geographical knowledge continued to be limited. In the northern section of the map we see the land of the Cimeiririm – a Hebrew word meaning 'darkness.'

This place was called 'Night Boundary' as opposed to 'Day Boundary' in Africa. It is certain that the Phoenicians were the first who made the effort to discover fairly far flung places by sea to further their trade. This is what is said of them:

> Advent'rous Tyre in ships was said to be
> The first that trusted faithless wind and sea.

It is believed they traded in lead and tin as early as 900B.C. with the Scilly Isles and possibly parts of Cornwall.

This transport was so important as to frighten one Cartheginian captain into sinking his ship so as not to reveal the Scillies to the Romans. On his return home he was rewarded for his loyalty with a new ship.

During the 12th/13th centuries, important maritime discoveries were made. These are related to the compass. The compass enabled adventures to the far reaches of the world. The Romans, Greeks, Norwegians, Spaniards, Portuguese, the British and others took part in these discoveries. These adventurers knew hardship and great danger and many lost their lives in the campaigns. Their names will live on for ever in the history books. Here are some of them – Pytheas, Eudoxes, Hauno, Marco Polo, Columbus, Pizarro, John & Sebastian Cabot, Vasco de Gama, Franklin, Abel Tasman, Drake, Sir Walter Raleigh, Dampier, Captain Cook, Bonganville, La Perouse, Captains Bligh and Flinders, Sir John Ross, Captain Wilks, Admiral Krusenstern, Dr. Livingstone and Stanley the Welshman.

By now nearly every part of the world is known to us. The map we have of the world is extremely accurate, particularly the coastlines. In fact so accurate that a ship can be sailed from this country to Australia – a voyage of about twelve thousand miles – without sighting land during a voyage of about three to four months and the time of sighting the port calculated almost to the minute.

The Jews, Arabs and others in olden times gave the name 'sea' to all large bodies of water; for example Lake Galilee – about thirteen miles long and five miles across was called the Tiberius Sea or the Galilean Sea. The Dead Sea which is only forty five miles long and ten miles wide was also called the Sodom Sea. The Mediterranean Sea which is about three thousand miles long was also called the Great Sea or the Eastern Sea. It was along this sea that Jonah started wandering and the Apostle Paul also sailed this sea on his journey to Rome. Yet another name was the Philistines' Sea as that nation lived along its shores.

But by now, further knowledge of the sea has increased people's perception of it. The Psalmist calls it 'the wide open sea.' In it, 'it is said, there are innumerable reptiles, beasts large and small.'

Nature does not have one element which impresses more on the human brain and the greatness of God than 'the wide open sea.' At times the sea is calm beneath the sun's rays or the moon's beams. Other times, its wide breast swells in waves moving slowly and majestically, breaking as white foam on the shore. On other occasions, it appears as if annoyed; its relentless waves beating against the rocks and shore with frightening strength and magnitude.

But if that be the appearance from land, what must be the experience for those 'who go down to the sea in ships and do business in great water?'

It is easier to imagine rather than to portray the feelings of the poor mariners when in tempestuous seas far from their homes and country – thousands of miles sometimes from land! Better pictures of the scene cannot be given than those of some of the Psalmists.

Ceiriog wrote of the ferocity of the sea in his ode to the sea 'Awdl y Môr' a piece of poetry written in strict rhythm. He talks about the often fatal effect of the stormy sea on vessels. We hear how the roar of the wind and the thrusting of the waves send horror through the soul. Although appearing shaky the vessels ride the mountainous waves. (Comparable to the Berwyn Mountains!!) Waves hit again and a boiling, cavernous 'valley' appears. The noise is overpowering. Death calls above the roar of the water for the mariner to enter the quiet land of the dead!

'THE WIDE OPEN SEA'

It is worthy of this name. Let us try to appreciate its vastness. The earth is approximately 196,633,356 miles square; and of these, 46.5 million are land and 150 million, sea. This approximates to 7 parts land and 23 parts sea assuming that the surface is made up of 30 parts or simply that two thirds of the earth is sea. It is feared that many in our midst have not begun to understand the vastness of the earth we dwell on. The word 'world' for many is the same as Liverpool or Wales or possibly a small part of the country. We hear about one old lady who apparently had not studied much geography saying; 'Our Robert is forever talking about going to Stralia; and they say this Stralia is very far – further than London so they say.' Surely it would be to our advantage to try and appreciate the magnitude of the sphere we occupy.

Recent discoveries prove without doubt that the sea is full of life. Of the three elements identified by the old philosophers, namely, fire, earth and water, it is in the water that the greatest amount of life is found. We see in the first chapter of Genesis that God created 'the large sea-horses and every reptile' which filled the waters with their species. The sea is full of animalculae (microscopic animals) which can only be seen when magnified. Despite their size, they accomplish great and important work as we shall realise later on. Naturalists believe that some of these tiny animalculae when coming into contact with each other or with something other than water, create a type of phosphorous. I have marvelled, many a night in mid-ocean, at the wonderful sight which appears on occasions. The sea around us seemed on fire and a fiery pathway, left by the ship, for a great distance, lit the sky above. Think of the hundreds of square miles of coral reefs – miles of coral built straight from the ocean floor to the surface. What can the sum total of these small creatures amount to and for how many years have they been striving to build even one of these numerous coral islands? The animalculae are so small, naturalists until recently thought that coral was a type of sea vegetable or so called polyparia.

It is assumed that all the chalk cliffs and marl beds found in parts of the world are memorials to these small creatures and a large number of islands, testament to their labour. They do not build them fully to the sea surface – but to about two or three feet below the surface. Therefore it is asked why so many of these Coral Islands are much higher than sea level? The common belief is that geological movements have raised the structures of the tiny builders above the surface. Then the sun works on the new island by throwing its' heat to break up and adapt the surface so that vegetation and trees grow on it. Following this, the wind also contributes by stealing various seeds from here and there which in time germinate without human intervention. (*Eight lines of Welsh poetry are included at this point in the original Welsh version. The lines state the great variety of grasses, reeds and vegetation, which grow as if by accident in the strangest places. This is seen as a wondrous process not able to be appreciated by a human.*)

THE DEPTH OF THE SEA

It is comparatively easy to measure the depth of the sea when not over 100 fathoms (600 feet) as in the St. George and English Channels. Actually these places, when compared to the Atlantic, Indian Sea and the Pacific, are not worthy of the noun 'sea.'

The common method of measuring depth is to attach lead (usually 28 pounds) to rope, letting the line run out until it is felt that the lead has hit the bottom. Wax is put on the lead so that a sample from the sea-bed will adhere to it. The certainty of the sea's depth is important to the sailor for him to detect the distance of his ship from land. And it is important for him to be aware of the nature of the sea-bed to understand the location of his ship. Because of this, sea depth and the nature of the sea-bed are carefully marked on charts. In some places, particularly close to land, clean sand is found; in other locations, sand and shells; again gravel, rocks and mud etc. And as previously suggested, the wax on the lead will bring a sample to the surface if the lead has not fallen on to a rock, and even then, the imprint of the rock will be on the wax on the lead. But when the water is very deep, it is difficult to measure depth because there is no certainty of knowing whether the lead has reached the bottom. And there are also currents in some areas carrying the line out even after the lead has reached the sea-bed. We can state that war ships of various countries have been diligently working for many years to try and measure ocean depths, in particular the Atlantic, and have been using different ways to achieve this goal. But, not for want of trying, the work of measuring the depth of the deepest parts of the ocean still has not been completed. It is said that in one valley, a near six mile line could not reach the bottom! But accurate measuring was achieved at a depth of 23,250 feet or nearly four and a half miles. And not only accurate measuring, but the acquisition of a sample which proved under magnification to contain, amongst other things, the most beautiful, small, delicate, shells. The general opinion is that these tiny creatures lived near the surface but dropped to the bottom after death.

It is virtually impossible to imagine the vastness of the sea-bed which is judged to be so big that it could accommodate all the dry land covered with a depth of a mile of water! If we could see it, it would be the strangest sight ever seen. Mr. Gladstone has called it the 'Home of Marvels.'

'A thousand fearful wrecks;
A thousand men that fishes gnaw'd upon;
Wedges of gold, great anchors, heaps of pears,
Inestimable stones, unvalued jewels,
All scatter'd in the bottom of the sea.'

BURIAL AT SEA

Burial on land is a serious affair, but even more serious at sea. It is an event not forgotten easily. We well remember the different times we had to bury at sea. But, in particular, I remember the last time I was responsible. Our ship at the time was near the Falkland Islands. The weather had been very stormy for days. On one of these days, our second mate lost his grip and fell from the top of the mast to the deck, and this proved fatal. All that could be done was to bury him with as much respect as possible in his watery grave. By the following morning, as was the norm, we had sewn him in a shroud and weighted his feet so that his body would sink to the bottom. And at eight thirty, orders were given to back the main yards and for all hands to come aft to bury the dead. Our crew numbered 25 and although many had been left 'like the chicks of an ostrich' and had not enjoyed our privileges, that morning, they carried their shipmate's body with great tenderness to be buried. After placing the body, covered by a British flag, on a plank of wood over the ship's side, the usual service proceeded until the point reached when 'we place him in the depths to return to ashes,' and the plank was raised and the remains of the co-mariner slipped to the depths to remain there until the day the sea will give up its dead.

(In the original version, a piece of poetry appears here reiterating what has already been said about the shroud/weights/plank etc.)

THE SALINITY OF THE SEA

Perhaps it would not be out of place to mention here a quotation from 'The Physical Geography of the Sea' by Captain Maury in relation to some of the elements present in sea salt:

The principal ingredients which chemists, by treating small samples of sea-water in the laboratory, have found in a thousand grains are:

Water	962.0grams
Chloride of Magnesium	5.4grams
Chloride of Potassium	0.4grams
Bromide of Magnesia	0.1grams
Sulphate of Magnesia	1.2grams
Sulphate of Lime	0.8grams
Carbonate of Lime	0.1grams
Leaving a residuum	2.0grams –1000

Consisting of sulphurated hydrogen gas, hydrochlorate of ammonies etc., in various quantities and proportions, according to the locality of the specimen.

It is said that there are no fewer than two hundred million tonnes of dissolved silver in the sea, and that the salt in it is sufficient to cover, at a thickness of a mile, several million square miles. It is also said that as salt does not expand the water, if all the salt was removed, the sea would not be any less. The question often asked is why is the sea salty? There are many opinions regarding the cause or causes of this. It is generally presumed that natural vegetable and animal wastage, phosphoric and ammonical substances, rocks and veins of salt in the sea are the natural causes of salinity.

Another question asked is – Was the sea salty from the onset? In response to this, one American authority says that in the 1st Chapter of Genesis, there is evidence to suggest that the sea was salty as early as the first day of creation. It is also said that the Hieroglyphics 'which are traced by the hand of Nature on the Geological Column,' prove the same thing.

EBB AND FLOW

The ebb and flow of the sea is one of the wonders of nature and very beneficial. Our ancestors could not appreciate the ebb and flow of the sea. Sir Isaac Newton, after studying the laws of gravitation and attraction, was the first to see that the moon was the chief cause of this phenomenon.

A HIGH WAY OF TRAFFIC

The seas are a worthwhile way for society to trade so that surplus in some countries can aid deficiency in others. Statistics show that on average, 502,396 tonnes were exported from this country monthly in the previous year – a total of 6,028,752 tonnes in a year. To give some idea of the value of the merchant ships of the main countries –see chart:

England	£112,000,000
France	10,200,000
Germany	14,100,000
Italy	4,500,000
Russia	2,450,000
America	9,200,000

These statistics show that ships carry food supplies worth £159,300,000 annually to Great Britain; £427,600,000 worth of other goods and £743,100,000 worth of imports and exports for this country annually. As many as 40,962 head of cattle were carried from America to Liverpool last year. Although figures and statistics are uninteresting to some of us, it is not uninteresting to learn how many ships and crews belong to our kingdom. We do not have later figures than those for 1889. But the number of steam ships in that year was 5,585 carrying 142,498 crew members. Sailing ships numbered 11,969 with crew members numbering 87,765. This made a total of 17,554 vessels and 230,265 mariners.

Let us hope, by now, that we have some appreciation of our dependency on ships and crew for our sustenance. And let us hope that 'those who go down to the sea in ships and do business in great waters,' are given our deepest sympathy and that we follow the good example of our fathers by giving them a worthy place in our prayers.

Thomas Owen, Liverpool

Appendix B

The letter titled 'Germany and England' appeared in the *Liverpool Daily Post*, April 30, 1910. I believe Captain Thomas Owen showed another aspect of his character and interests in this letter to the Editor in the Spring of 1910 when there was considerable noise and thunder regarding the aggressive policies of Germany. Note the ideas of the old master-mariner from Minafon, Tudweiliog on trading matters, the lack of interest shown by the British in learning foreign languages and the madness of nationalism in Britain and Germany which, in due course, was responsible for World War One, 1914–1918.

Liverpool Daily Post. 30th April, 1910, by J. Owen.

GERMANY AND ENGLAND

To the Editor of the Post and Mercury

Sir, – In submitting a few remarks on some aspects of the Germany versus England question may I preface my observations by saying that for forty years I have been moving about Continental ports, and during that period a great change has taken place. One big difference has come in the substitution of steamers for sailing vessels, but a more important change is evidenced in the enormous number of foreign ensigns in every port as compared with what there were, say, in the 60s. Before the passing of the absurd Trade Marks Act, continental goods came to England in British ships, and were sent abroad again in British ships. Now, the Continental nations have gradually built up their own lines, and we must begin to look things in the face. There are things that have contributed to this, and among them is the crowd of young men coming over from Germany and Austria to learn our language and our business methods, and to pick our brains, distributing themselves through our ports and commercial cities.

Who is this young invader of our commerce? He is the eldest son of his father in Germany, who is a merchant there, say butter merchant. His age is twenty, he had had a good commercial education, with a smattering of the English language. As soon as he arrives at his destination – shall we say Liverpool? – he presents his credentials to some German commercial gentlemen, from whom he will receive the names of all butter business houses in the city, and possibly an introduction to the head of each firm, and in due time he presents himself very innocently(?) before the head of one of the firms with a plausible tale in broken English, that he has come to England to learn the language, and is prepared to give his services as a clerk in his office for twelve or eighteen months *without any salary*, with the result that he is there and then engaged, the partners in the firm complimenting themselves that they have done good business by securing the services of a clerk for eighteen months without any salary whatever. When his time is up the young man will leave, without any monetary consideration, of course, but with a knowledge of the business and a full list of the firm's customers, all of which will be returned to the very best account when he gets into his father's office in Germany. Result, the firm at Liverpool will find that there is a leak somewhere in their business, and we shall call this leak No. 1.

Leak No. 2. – We have heard on several occasions merchants aboard complaining that they cannot get English manufacturers to pack their goods in a manner most suitable to the buyers, and should they write the British merchant on the subject their answer invariably would be that the goods were packed as they had been always accustomed to here; while the foreign manufacturer would not only pack their goods according to the buyers' wishes, but would also manufacture them just as required, irrespective of what they had been doing previously.

Leak No. 3. – Let us imagine two letters being delivered together at a merchant's office, say in France, both of them bearing quotations for the same goods. The merchant opens the first letter, and finds that it is written in English, a language he but imperfectly understands. He further finds that the prices are given in pounds, shillings, pence, and farthings, for weights of 112 lbs. in the hundredweight, containing four quarters of 28 lbs. and that the pound has 16 ounces! He puts that letter aside and opens the other, and perceives that it is written in French (notwithstanding that it has come from Germany), and should the quotations not be in French currency (which would not at all be likely) they are on the decimal system, identical with French coinage, viz., 100 pfennings to the mark, like 100 centimes to the franc, and the weights and measures are the same in both France and Germany, so that the French merchant can readily grasp the quotations without having to undertake the laborious calculations necessary in case of the British quotations. The natural result will be, in nine cases out of ten, that the order for the goods will pass to Germany. It has always been a great wonder to many, yea, all, who have seriously considered the matter, that we in Britain have adhered so long to our most complicated system of money, weights, and measures, instead of adopting the decimal and metric system, which has been long in vogue in the principal commercial countries of the world.

The English language is proudly claimed by Englishmen to be good enough for anybody, and most continental business men learn it. But we need to reciprocate – or retaliate – by teaching our young men some other language than English. We are being told that Germany can build Dreadnoughts more quickly than we can, which, if true, is a compliment to us in one way, for we have exported naval architects to Germany to teach our rivals, who, when they have done with the Britisher, 'scrap' him, and he goes home. Besides, the Kaiser is an admiral of our Fleet, and enjoys all the privileges attaching to that rank. But a Britisher is not allowed to witness – at close quarters – the launch of a battleship at Hamburg! Have we no foreigners in the reserved enclosures when our ships are launched? But what a miserable business it is, this perpetual war of armaments. We are almost of the same blood as the Germans; we are, in the main, Protestants as they are, against the amusing claims of Rome, we are all supposed to worship the same God, while dishonouring Him in our bloodthirsty rivalry. Is there no means of pacific arrangements, or are we all bitten with the insane desire to take our brother's life as well as his goods? –

Yours & c.
Minavon
27 April 1910

Appendix C

BRIGANTINE
*A two-masted vessel square-rigged on the foremast, fore-and-aft on
the mainmast, although the original type of brigantine carried
square-sail on the main topmast also*

BRIG
A two-masted vessel, square-rigged on both masts

TOPSAIL SCHOONER
*A vessel with two or more masts. Fore-and-aft rigged on all masts
with the addition of square topsails on the foremast*

BARQUENTINE
*A vessel with three or more masts. Square-rigged on her foremast
and fore-and-aft on all others*

BARQUE
A vessel of three or more masts, square-rigged on all masts but the aftermost, which is fore-and-aft rigged

FULL-RIGGED SHIP
A three-masted vessel with square-sail on all masts. Four and five-masted full-rigged ships have been known

References

Chapter 1 – Roots

P. 11 ¹ Many lives were lost on the Welsh coast between 1859 and 1864, besides several on the night of the *Royal Charter* storm. See Parliamentary Commission, 1858–9, 1.244. For further details of the *Royal Charter* storm see R. R. Williams, 'Anglesey and the loss of the *Royal Charter*' T.C.H.M. (1969); Alexander McKee, *The Golden Wreck* (1961), and T. Llew Jones, *Ofnadwy Nos* (1971).

P. 12 ² The accounts for 1841, 1851, 1861, 1871 and 1881 in Gwynedd Archives, Caernarfon; Llaniestyn Parish records, xpe/41; Tudweiliog Parish records, xpe/45. Richard Williams and Jane Williams, Penyberth (Miss Sarah Roberts' grandmother) were brother and sister, and the children of Porthdinllaen Farm.

P. 14 ³ *O Bwllheli i Bendraw'r Byd* (1979), *Porthmadog Ships* (1974) and *Ships and Seamen of Anglesey* (1974).

P. 14 ⁴ My friend, Dr. Lewis Lloyd, who has researched much of Pwllheli history suggests that it was the school in Penlan St. that was advertised in the thirties. e.g. Jan. 1835: 'Miss Edwards respectfully informs her friends and the public that she will be happy to receive into her establishment a few YOUNG LADIES whom she will instruct in every branch of liberal and finished education, uniting the advantages of school with the comforts of home.'

P. 14 ⁵ *Baner ac Amserau Cymru.* June 21st 1876.

P. 15 ⁶ *Antelope.* Official number 4168, 9/1851, Caernarfon. (Gwynedd Archive Services.)

P. 16 ⁷ *Lady Louisa Pennant,* Gwynedd Archives Service, Llangefni. There is some history regarding the *Lady Louisa*

*Pennan*t in my piece about Captain David Roberts, Bangor in *Meistri'r Moroedd* (1978), 131-2.

P. 17 [8] *Collina*, no. 1563, 9/1854, G.A.S., Caernarfon.

P. 17 [9] Lloyd's Register.

P. 17 [10] Account regarding the application for his ticket in the archives of the National Maritime Museum, Greenwich.

P. 18 [11] G.A.S., Caernarfon. XM/5009, XS/2405.

P. 18 [12] There is more information regarding Captain Thomas Williams, Liverpool's voyages in the book *Oes Aur y Llongau Hwyliau*, being published at present by the Welsh University Press.

P. 18 [13] Kellock's Papers (uncatalogued) in N.M.M. Greenwich.

P. 18 [14] There is more discussion regarding the history of the clubs in 2 books: *Oes Aur y llongau Hwyliau* and *The Owners*.

P. 19 [15] Captain Richard Richards was the son of the ships' carpenter, Evan Richards, Penlan, Barmouth.

P. 19 [16] Certificate of discharge G.A.S., Caernarfon. XM/5009.

P. 20 [17] Ibid.

P. 20 [18] I am indebted to Miss G. Williams and to Miss M. Williams, Rhos on Sea for the information regarding their grandfather, Captain Owen Williams, Beaumaris, master of the *William Leavit*.

P. 21 [19] Aled Eames, *Shipmaster*, 'The Life and Letters of Captain Robert Thomas, Llandwrog and Liverpool. 1843–1903'. (G.A.S.)

P. 22 [20] Ibid.

P. 25 [21] Parliamentary Papers 1880. LXXIV, 801 et seq. The account of the British magistrate in Callao came to a head suddenly on April 14th 1880: 'The establishment of a blockade of the port of Callao by the Chilean forces, and the imminent bombardment of the place, render it necessary to bring this report to an abrupt conclusion, with the view of despatching it at the first opportunity'.

Chapter 2 – The *Cambrian Monarch*

P. 27 [1] See *Victorian Shipbuilding in Southampton* by Adrian Rance. I am grateful to Mr Rance, the curator of Southampton Museum, not only for a copy of his book, but also for notes on the ships built by T. R. Oswald for other Liverpool companies.

P. 29 [2] The Diary, Monday, 20th March 1882.

P. 32 [3] I must thank Mr M. K. Stammers, Liverpool Maritime Museum, for giving up his precious time to copy the details of the Cambrian ships from the ships' register for me, as he is very busy with the problems of the new maritime museum.

P. 41 [4] P.R.O. BT 31/5872/41230.

Chapter 3 – Women and the Sea

P. 50 [1] Horace Beck, *Folklore and the Sea*. The American Maritime Library, Vol. vi, Mystic Seaport (1973), 279-313.

P. 51 [2] The Voyage of the 'Donald McKay' 14th July 1864 – 17th July 1865. The details are in the ship's log which are currently in the N.M.M. archives. Captain Richards' address at the time was 22, Woodville Terrace, Everton. 12 of the passengers died on the way out, 4 being soldiers.

P. 51 [3] Miss Sarah Roberts, Ala Road, Pwllheli, was kind enough to give me a copy of this delightful booklet. It was published by H. Humphries, Letter-Press, Lithographic and Copperplate printer, Caernarfon 1856. J. Roberts, who wrote the booklet after he came to Britain from Australia in the ship *Orwell* is prepared to recommend the ship *John Davies*. He was coming home to live in Menai Bridge, and the Davies family had the pleasure of reading the praise for his ships.

P. 51 [4] 52 children, mostly under 12 months old, died from chicken pox on the first voyage of the well-known ship *Marco Polo* belonging to the Black Ball line, on the way out to Australia in 1852, a very fast passage under Captain Bully Forbes.

P. 51 5 Christopher Lloyd, *The British Seaman,* (1970). P. 224.

P. 52 6 Aled Eames, *Ships and Seamen of Anglesey.* 495-498; A. Eames, *Meistri'r Moroedd,* 167-175.

P. 53 7 Aled Eames, *Porthmadog Ships.* 400-417.

P. 54 8 Aled Eames, *Machlud Hwyliau'r Cymru.* (1984).

P. 55 9 Ibid.

P. 56 10 Aled Eames, *Meistri'r Moroedd* 209, 199-210.

P. 56 11 Ibid. 136-146.

P. 57 12 Ibid. 66-75.

P. 57 13 I am grateful to Mrs Elinor Ellis, Heswall, Wirral, the grandaughter of Captain and Mrs Griffith Jones, *Langdale* for letting me see the diary and photographs she has kept so carefully. Her uncle, Captain John Griffith Jones, the son of Captain Griffith Jones was good enough to share his own memories of living on the *Langdale.*

P. 60 14 I have new information regarding the voyages of Captain William Williams and his wife thanks to Mrs Riby Williams, Weymouth, who was a good friend of many years. See also *Meistri'r Moroedd* 55 and 66.

P. 61 15 See *Y Wawr,* Summer 1983 for further information regarding the 2 Mrs Meredith.

P. 62 16 Papurau Rhyddgaer, Llangefni. G.A.S. The letter is reproduced verbatim.

P. 62 17 John P. Parker, *Cape Breton Ships and Men,* 160, 162-164.

Chapter 4 – The Diary

P. 65 1 Lloyd's weekly shipping index Aug. 19th 1881.
Cambrian Monarch, British ship, sailed Newport May 12th, arrived Sydney, N.S.W. Aug.12th.

P. 65 2 This document is under cases about the tickets, 'only mate', 'mate' and 'master' in the N.M.M. archives. This large collection is currently in the 'Brass Foundry' Henry VIIIth at Woolwich. His master's ticket number is 91797 and on this copy is noted 'I hereby certify that this certificate, which is granted under the 139th section of the Merchant Shipping Act 1854, is a True Copy of the original now on record in this office, General Register and Record office of Shipping and Seamen, fifth day of August 1882.' According to the original ticket Thomas Owen passed his master's ticket in Feb. 1873: 'Issued at Pwllheli, the port of Caernarfon on the 20th day of Feb. 1873, signed R. Evans, Dy. Sup. M. Marine'. Thomas Owen had passed the exam in Liverpool on 3rd Feb. 1873 and gave his address at the time as '12 Windsor Street, Liverpool'. In his application for his first mate's ticket two years earlier his address was '1, Edmund Street, Liverpool'.

P. 66 3 In one of the papers that is in the possession of Mrs Elinor Ellis her mother, Moraned, described the cabin on the *Langdale* where she and her brother, John Griffith Jones, lived whilst sailing the seas with their parents, Captain and Mrs Griffith Jones, Pwllheli. 'We had a big cabin, as big as your sitting room and dining room together, with a few separate cabins leading from it'. One gets some idea of the living quarters of these large ships by going on board the *Cutty Sark* at Greenwich. There is an excellent description of the life as described to a child in J. Ifor Davies', *Growing up Among Sailors*. G.A.S. 1983.

P. 66 4 Kellock Mss. (uncatalogued), N.M.M. Greenwich. 'List of effects of Master of the Ship Langdale', signed by Captain J. Hunter.

P. 67 5 Lloyds W.S.I. Jan. 18th 1882. *Cambrian Monarch*, Owen. British ship, Sydney New South Wales. September 25th Arrived San Francisco, December 9th, 1881. L.W.S.I. Feb. 10th 1882. *Cambrian Monarch*, Owen, British ship. San Francisco sailed Feb. 4th for Queenstown.

P. 67 [6] Photo. page 37.

P. 68 [7] We do not know why Thomas Owen is using a crutch. Maybe this is why Ellen mentioned that 'Tom's health was better once they were sailing for home.' He was quite ill in ''Frisco before leaving.' Maybe Thomas Owen was suffering from gout.

Of course the crutch could be there because he hurt his leg on the ship. Maybe this happened during the storm that wrecked the cabin.

P. 68 [8] Photo. page 108.

P. 69 [9] We saw that Captain Owen was one of the masters who took part in the temperance meeting on board *Malabar* chaired by Captain David Evans, Nefyn, and Captain Robert Thomas, Llandwrog, on the east coast of South America in 1875. In the account of his death in *Y Drysorfa* it says that Captain Owen was one of the Welsh captains who held religious meetings on board his ship. 'He kept an eye on his sailors and would not allow bad language on his ship. It is worth noting that his ship was often used for services whilst in port. The captain undertook to look after his fellow mariners, and heaven alone knew how much help he gave to many sailors, young and old, so keeping them on the straight and narrow.' (*Y Drysorfa*, XCII, October 1921, p. 391)

P. 69 [10] A. Eames, *Shipmaster*. 'The Life and Letters of Captain Robert Thomas, Llandwrog'. (G.A.S 1980).

P. 70 [11] James Fell, *British Merchant Seamen in San Francisco*.

P. 72 [12] Remember that the Captain or the mate had to deal with any accident or ill health and their only reference was Seaman's *Medical Dictionary*. See J. Ifor Davies' *Growing up Among Sailors* p. 176 for a good account of Captain Davies having to put stitches in his own neck.

P. 74 [13] 12th May 1881.

P. 74 [14] Sept. 1881. Ellen Owen wrote on the cover of her diary that she was keeping the logged distances in red, but from March 12th onwards she adds the figures at the end of the daily record. For convenience the miles are in brackets from Feb. 4th to March 1st.

P. 76 [15] The *Cambrian Monarch* shipwright and brother-in-law to Thomas Owen. The sermons of the late Rev. John Jones, Talysarn together with a preface by the editor, were published under the auspices of the Rev. Griffith Parry, Llanrwst by Thomas Gee of Denbigh in 1869. There were 670 pages and over 50 John Jones sermons on various testaments. (P. 106 *Pregethau'r Diweddar John Jones, Talysarn*).

P. 76 [16] You can see the effects of the weather on Ellen Owens' handwriting in the diary; the 'light winds' and the 'pitching' in Feb. were not as bad as the rough weather in March. e.g. Thursday 16th March when writing is very difficult indeed.

P. 77 [17] The equator.

P. 78 [18] The Doldrums. i.e. between the northern and southern trade winds, near the equator. This was very important to sailing ships which could be caught without any wind at all for some time. It is worth noting the memories of Captain David Roberts, Dolgellau when sailing the Atlantic ocean from Antwerp to San Francisco i.e. a different direction from the voyage described by Ellen Owen. He claimed it was easier to cross the doldrums in the Pacific ocean than in the Atlantic. He was one of the most successful captains of the large sailers, being master of the *Kirkcudbrightshire* for many years.

'We soon picked up the North East Trade Winds, which blow steadily all the year round varying little in force or direction. These winds carry us 7 degrees north of the equator, the ship averaging 250 miles a day. When drawing towards the end of the Trade Winds the wind gradually fell light, the sky became overcast and the sea oily and sluggish.

All these signs are well known to the experienced mariner, being certain indication that they are approaching the dreaded doldrums. If there is a part of the ocean that is more disliked than others by the sailing ship man it is this belt of calms, averaging between two and three hundred miles across, lying near the equator between N.E. and S.E. trade winds. Generally speaking the heat is extreme, the wind, if any, is variable coming in gusts. This means trying work for the crew, trimming the sails to every breath of wind. The officer of the watch knows full well that by the time he has finished trimming the sails the wind will be gone, but he must keep at it. That is the only way to work a sailing ship through the doldrums. Sometimes there is a little variation in the way of heavy wind squalls and torrential rain lasting about 10 minutes but invariably followed by another calm spell. During the heavy rain every outlet for the water was closed, and the sailors, stripped to the waist, enjoyed a thoroughly good scrubbing. This was a luxury in which sailors rarely indulged.'

See *Maritime Wales*. No. 8 1984.

P. 79 [19] Auction. Clothes, tobacco and things bought from the chandlers by the captain before sailing. Jones 'Golden Goat' was well known in Cardiff, not only as a ship's chandler, but also as a meeting place for the captains. This is the sort of thing that happened all over the world. A sale of clothes and artefacts belonging to a sailor who had died fetched good prices as the money went to the family, but when the sale benefited the captain as this did it is surprising that the price paid for Ellen Owen's socks was so high.

P. 79 [20] 'Slops' was the name given to clothes sold on the naval and the merchant ships. The word probably came originally from 'sloppe', an old English word for trousers or clothes worn by mariners in the navy. It was being used as early as the 17th century.

P. 81 [21] Pitcairn Island, 25 degees, 3 minutes south. 130 degrees 8 minutes West.

P. 82 [22] The *Golden Gate* was a ship built by Thomas Royden of Liverpool and belonging to Cotesworth, Lyne, Tower Buildings, Liverpool. 899 t.195.6/33.7/21. She arrived in San Francisco on Jan. 2nd 1882 and she had some damage from strong northern winds on Jan. 12th. L.W.S.T. Feb. 10th 1882.

P. 83 [23] Old mariners still make mats, one of the main hobbies at sea. Newborough, Anglesey was at one time well known for the mats made by sailors.

P. 84 [24] This is a day when we see the effect of the weather on Ellen's writing. I believe that Ellen Owen's description of the storms from March 15th onwards describes the experiences of generations of mariners, the dangers high above the decks, fighting strong winds, cold, heavy seas and darkness, whilst the ship rolls and everyone is soaked to the skin. At times like these it was easy to wish for dry land and a warm bed, even in the poorest cottage.

P. 84 [25] 'Cors Iago', the building near the 'Felin', 'Tyddyn Mawr' and 'Tyddyn Sander', Tudweiliog, where Thomas Owen had his new home, 'Minafon' built at the end of the voyage.

P. 85 [26] This shows that Ellen did not make the first voyage in the *Cambrian Monarch*. He had left the *British India* in 1880 and thus there must have been another voyage before this one.

P. 85 [27] By this time Ellen had developed the same feeling for the ship as she had for the animals on the farm, or for a child. I have heard many tales of captains talking to their ships and murmuring 'keep at it, sweetheart, we must keep going'. The fact that Ellen says that the *Cambrian Monarch* was a good ship in stormy weather reiterates the opinion of many that T. R. Oswald was a very good builder of ships.

P. 85 [28] ? foggy.

P. 85 [29] Although the weather was dreadful Ellen and the crew were prepared to accept this as it meant they were travelling fast and in the right direction i.e. HOME. Captain Owen knew well that clashes with other ships or icebergs had finished many a ship round the Horn.

P. 86 [30] I expect they had the 'Patent Log' on the *Cambrian Monarch* as invented by Thomas Walker in 1861, developed from the work of Walker's uncle Edward Massey from the log line that was towed behind the ship. This turned a wheel attached to the tape measure. By 1884 Walker's 'Patent Log' took the name 'Cherub', starting a service that was very important to many mariners.

P. 86 [31] The San Francisco furniture.

P. 86 [32] This is a high salary in relation to £18 a month usually paid to the masters of sailing ships at the beginning of the 19th century. e.g. In 1907, Captain Robert Jones, Amlwch, master of *Talus* was paid £18 a month.

P. 86 [33] Captain James McGill, previous master of *Carnarvonshire*, a wooden ship belonging to the company of Captain Thomas Williams and later the *Cambrian Princess*. McGill, a native of Glasgow, was 44 years old when he sailed for Callao on the 20th Jan. 1874. By 1882 he was probably marine superintendent and part owner of the Cambrian ships.

P. 86 [34] By 1884 Thomas Williams fleet had reduced to 7 ships; *Cambrian Monarch, Cambrian Prince, Cambrian Princess, Cambrian Queen* and the wooden ships, *Carnarvonshire, Eastern Light* and the *William Leavit*.

P. 87 [35] Squall. Sailing out against the strong east winds was much harder than the voyage home, so you can understand Ellen Owen using the words 'poor things' regarding the ship they saw. Note the J. W. Peters diary in my book *Machlud Hwyliau'r Cymru* (1984).

P. 88 [36] In bad weather the work of the helmsman was very hard. See Alan Villiers' *Voyaging with the Wind,* and Commodore Gerald N. Jones' claim about Harry Hughes from Amlwch who was lost from the *Ladye Doris* in *Ships and Seamen of Anglesey* P. 259.

P. 88 [37] After reading 670 pages.

P. 90 [38] Attendance.

P. 91 [39] They were expecting to pick up the 'Trades'.

P. 92 [40] This was the usual procedure. The captains knew the ship was expected to look good, being spruced up on the homeward voyage, so reaching her final port looking smart and in 'shipshape'.

P. 92 [41] See P. 10.

P. 93 [42] With flags.

P. 96 [43] Seeing another woman was always something special and this note, after all the cold followed by intense heat, was part of the seafaring women's lives. The terrible loneliness, month after month and only the sea and the enclosed cabin, which first seen in port seemed large.

P. 97 [44] See note 18 above.

P. 97 [45] Ellen Owen's sister; Tyddyn Mawr was the next farm to Cors Iago.

P. 100 [46] One of the problems of iron sailing ships was finding the opportunity to clean the keel and the ship's sides, although paint makers were starting to produce the type of paint that made the voyage of the *Merioneth* possible in 1878/8. See *Shipmaster.* P. 163/4.

P. 102 [47] Many ship masters were frustrated when they arrived off the southern Irish coast having had a fast voyage until then. See *Shipmaster* P. 142/48 and the letters of Captain Robert Thomas to his daughter.

P. 102 [48] The Azores or the 'Western Islands', the name the old mariners gave them; about 900 miles west of Lisbon, 33 degrees 44 minutes N., 25 degrees 40 minutes West.

P. 103 [49] It was routine for ships nearing the end of their voyage to call at Queenstown (Cobh) or Falmouth 'for orders' as to which port they should unload their cargo.

P. 105 [50] They had taken 113 days on the voyage home. Lubbock in *The Last of the Windjammers* (2) referred to the length of time of the voyages. It was comparatively fast, underlining the achievement of Captain Robert Thomas in 1887/8 sailing from Cardiff to San Francisco in 90 days, returning in 95, the fastest voyage ever in this type of ship. It shows the *Cambrian Monarch* was unlucky in taking a week on the last stage of her journey.

Chapter 4 – Minafon

P. 106 [1] L.W.S.I. 23rd June 1882. *Cambrian Monarch*, British ship, Owen. San Francisco Feb. 4th for Limerick, arr. June 13.

P. 106 [2] L.W.S.I. 21st July 1882. *Cambrian Monarch*. Br. ship. Owen. Limerick. Arr. London 18th July.

P. 106 [3] David Thomas, *Hen Longau Sir Caernarfon*. (1952). 170.

P. 109 [4] My italics (i.e. Aled Eames).

P. 110 [5] Gwynedd Archives Services.

P. 111 [6] J. Glyn Davies, *Cerddi Huw Puw*.

P. 112 [7] P.R.O. BT31.

P. 112 [8] J. Glyn Davies, *Cerddi Huw Puw*.

P. 114 [9] National Maritime Museum, Kellock. Mss. These are the details of the ships bought by Robert Owen & Co. According to Lloyd's Register the *Invermore* was a steel barque, 1600 tons, 246/37.9/22.1, built in Belfast by Workman, Clark and Co., in 1891; *Centurion*, steel ship, 1828 tons, 257.1/39/22.7, built by Russell & Co., Greenock in 1891; *Langdale*, iron ship, 2047 tons, 275/40.1/24.2, built by W. H. Potter and Son, Liverpool, 1885.

P. 114 [10] P.R.O. 31/6373/65536.

P. 116 [11] C.A.L. *Carnarvon Bay*. N.M.M. Greenwich.

P. 116 [12] This painting, which is now in the possession of Mrs Elinor Ellis, was a present from Captain Griffith Jones to his wife after she joined the ship in Antwerp. It is believed that Captain Jones saw a picture of the *Melpomene* by H. Mohrmann, Antwerp and he decided to commission the painting from him. Mrs Elinor Ellis has a postcard of the *Melpomene* and the captain has written on the back 'The captain of this ship is a friend of mine. Put it in your album'.

P. 117 [13] Details of this application for his captain's ticket, now in the N.M.M. Greenwich.

P. 119 [14] During this voyage to Hongay, China, Captain Griffith Jones had the experience of being attacked by pirates in the South China Seas. I understood from Captain John Griffith Jones, his son, that a squall of heavy rain came down and gave *Langdale* a chance to escape.

P. 119 [15] In the postcard sent to his son it shows in black ink where the *Langdale* was damaged.

P. 121 [16] P.R.O. BT 31/16373/65536.

P. 121 [17] Ibid.

P. 122 [18] Aled Eames, *Ships and Seamen of Anglesey*.

P. 122 [19] 'Journal of Commerce' Aug. 5th.1916, when the prices dropped between 1911 and 1916. Also, Kellock's Mss. in N.M.M.Greenwich.

P. 122 [20] The *Talus* was sold for £21,000 in 1916, at £10.14.0 a ton.

The *Gwydyr Castle* was sold by Robert Thomas in 1898 for £8,000, and then by Roberts, Owen & Co, in 1916, for £18,500. I do not have the prices of the *Oweenee* or the *Langdale* in 1916.

P. 123 [21] The Tudweiliog school headmaster's books and the school records.

I am very grateful to the present headmaster, Mr Pritchard, for his help and welcome to Mr Bryn Parry and myself in Tudweiliog school.

P. 124 [22] *Y Traethodydd* 1893. XLIX. 22-28. See appendix A.
P. 125 [23] *Y Drysorfa* XCII. OCT. 1921. 393.
P. 125 [24] *Herald.* June 17th 1919.